MAN ON THE ROCK

Also by Michael Freedland

Al Jolson (later and in the US, *Jolson*)
Irving Berlin (later, *Salute to Irving Berlin*)
James Cagney (in the US, *Cagney*)
Fred Astaire
Sophie: The Story of Sophie Tucker
Jerome Kern
Errol Flynn (in the US, *The Two Lives of Errol Flynn*)
Gregory Peck
Maurice Chevalier
Peter O'Toole
The Warner Brothers
So Let's Hear the Applause: The Story of the Jewish Entertainer
Katharine Hepburn
The Goldwyn Touch
The Secret Life of Danny Kaye
Dustin
Leonard Bernstein
Kenneth Williams
Sean Connery
André Previn
Music Man
Bob Hope
Bing Crosby
All The Way: A Biography of Frank Sinatra
Michael Caine
Doris Day
Some Like It Cool: The Charmed Life of Jack Lemmon
Liza with a 'Z': The Traumas and Triumphs of Liza Minnelli
Witch Hunt in Hollywood
The Men Who Made Hollywood
Judy Garland: The Other Side of the Rainbow
Elvis Memories

With Morecambe and Wise
There's No Answer to That

With Walter Scharf
Composed and Conducted by Walter Scharf

Memoirs
Confessions of a Serial Biographer

MAN ON THE ROCK

MAYOR SOLOMON LEVY AND THE JEWS OF GIBRALTAR

MICHAEL FREEDLAND

VALLENTINE MITCHELL
LONDON • CHICAGO, IL

First published in paperback in 2016 by Vallentine Mitchell

Catalyst House,
720 Centennial Court, Centennial Park
Elstree, Herts WD6 3SY, UK

814 N Franklin Street
Chicago, Illinois
60610, USA

www.vmbooks.com

first published in hardback in 2013

British Library Cataloguing in Publication Data
An entry can be found on request

ISBN 978 0 85303 857 3 (cloth)
ISBN 978 0 85303 997 6 (paper)
ISBN 978 0 85303 867 2 (ebook)

Library of Congress Cataloging in Publication Data
An entry can be found on request

Printed by Independent Publishers Group, Chicago, IL

Author's Note

Every biography of this kind is necessarily a collaborative effort between author and subject. They won't always see eye to eye and that is how it should be. In this case, the finished product includes the fruit of a few decisions which reflected the preferences of the subject over that of the author. Some readers may feel the result betrays the odd gap. But they should rest assured that this is the story as Momy – and the family that loves him – wanted it to be told.

Michael Freedland, 2013

FOR FIONA, DANI AND JONATHAN

whose support has been unwavering and
who cherish the memory and love
for their mother, my wife Sara,
as I do myself.

CONTENTS

ACKNOWLEDGEMENTS

This has been a tour of discovery of a man who loves so many things – his wife and family above all, his country and its Queen close behind, and a vast number of enthusiasms that occupy his life along with everything else.

In a series of long interviews, covering more than 100 hours, Momy Levy talked to me about his life and his loves.

He particularly loves people – some of whom shared their thoughts and memories of him with me for this study of the Man on the Rock. They include:

Above all, his charming wife Sarah, who told me about living with a man who doesn't know how to sit still – unless it is to watch *Newsnight* or the Sunday morning political programmes on television. She is a perfect hostess, a fact which she has demonstrated to me so beautifully time and time again.

My thanks, too, to His Excellency The Governor of Gibraltar, Vice Admiral Sir Adrian Johns, who not only spoke to me at length, but gave me a personal guided tour of his 'palace' at what is engagingly called 'the Convent'. His kindness is so much appreciated.

Momy's two brothers, Abraham and James, were always helpful.

Then there were his close friends, Robert Seruya and Abie Massias, the local communal rabbi, Ronnie Hassid, the leader of Gibraltar's Opposition, Danny Feetham and the journalist Joe Garcia.

And one mustn't forget the literally hundreds of people to whom I have been introduced in my walks with him through Main Street who simply call out, 'Hi, Momy!' So Hi to them all. As high and as strong as the Rock of Gibraltar.

PLATES

A MAN CALLED MOMY

Momy is the embodiment of everything that is British and everything that it is to be a British Gibraltarian.

Danny Anthony Feetham

They call him Momy. Everyone calls him Momy. You could, of course, argue that it has a certain resonance about it and that it trips more easily off the tongue than the name on his birth certificate, Solomon. If someone called him Solomon Levy, Momy would probably put in a call to his solicitor.

Just as in the iconic movie, set in the city just over the sea, everyone knew Rick, so everyone in Solomon Levy's home town knows Momy.

Man on the Rock? To some, this former mayor of the territory IS the Rock, as stable as the Rock of Gibraltar, as dependable as that millennia-old stick of granite which we are talking about, the one protruding into the sea, surrounded on three sides by the kingdom of Spain that Momy likes so much, although he would take up arms to prevent it running own his tiny country, a place which he loves with a passion few could emulate.

In some ways, you can understand that. Even though the policemen speak Spanish, they look as if they have just walked out of a British country police station (providing you can find such a place) or even Scotland Yard. The soldiers of the Gibraltar Regiment look like any other British troops.

As the Governor, Sir Adrian Johns, put it to me:

> There's no doubt that [the Gibraltarians] are British. But they're not English and they're not part of the UK, but they're a very different Mediterranean people, the Gibraltarian British. Momy is a great sort of example of that, actually. You can't touch him for his Britishness and his loyalty to the monarchy. He speaks Spanish, he used to love bullfighting, and this sort of southern Mediterranean culture is imbued in the people there.

Momy and the Governor are good friends, which is why they and their wives would go together to one of the local kosher restaurants. Sir Adrian said:

> He was one of the first people I shook hands with apart from the great and the good when I arrived in Gibraltar. There he was, larger than life, walking across just as we happened to come to the top. And we were walking up from the parliament building where I'd given my sort of swearing-in speech in full regalia and Momy was there, presenting me with a tie – as he does with everyone here, the Union flag and the Gibraltar flag crossed. And you know, just then, I realized that he was someone who epitomized what Gibraltar was all about, this passion about themselves and being British and the Rock and fiercely loyal and fiercely defensive about who they are and what they have. Very admirable.

And, said the Governor, it is obvious that he is 'absolutely wedded to the Rock and I think, you know, his enthusiasm for that sort of cascades off into other people as well'. He says he sees that on Saturday mornings when he and his wife 'perambulate down with everyone else, for a coffee and [to] talk to people'. And he knows the Momy that other people know so well: 'You know, you never see Momy looking slightly down at heel; you know, never without beautiful bow ties. He makes the effort. Lovely.'

As we shall see, to say that Momy enjoys being part of Gibraltar is an understatement, as is his love of simply being Jewish. He is not afraid to let everyone know how important both those features of his life are. Sometimes, loyalty to the Crown is the one that gets the publicity. And, now in his late 70s, he is content to proclaim: 'British I was born and British I will die.' For him, the Queen is the symbol of everything that is good about Britain. As he told me: 'If the Queen wasn't in England, it wouldn't be England. She has made Britain what it is and I'll do anything for the Queen. I'm a great monarchist', he stresses – as if that needed stressing.

If the Queen said he should put on show a picture of himself wearing his bowler hat and little else, he would surely abandon his views on elegance and agree to the command – walking down Gibraltar's Main Street to do so.

'In fact', he says, 'I belong to a society which is called the Constitution of Monarchy Association and I contribute £50 to £100 a year', and he backs this up with a poster bearing those words about being born and dying British, in his office. What's more, for Diamond Jubilee year he installed a huge hoarding outside that office, showing the Queen looking her best in a yellow dress and hat. That cost him £2,000 and a row over planning permission, but he says it was worth it. Anything that can proclaim his loyalty has a value that is beyond price.

His attitude to the monarch has long been a subject for discussion among the good and great in Gibraltar. His younger brother James, a QC and head of the Rock's Jewish community, is totally with him in sharing his sense of national loyalty. 'I wouldn't put up a banner outside my offices', he comments:

> I don't express my views in that way. But I tell you that his love for Britain is not misplaced at all. Gibraltar has benefited hugely from the British government and the British government have benefited hugely from Gibraltar. But the best relations ... *are* the ones that allow both sides to benefit, in which one doesn't lose.

Momy will say that his lack of what one might call shyness is for the good cause that is his love for his country. As his son Isaac put it to me: 'He gets terribly excited when he sees his name in a newspaper.' And Momy will agree with that. 'Publicity? I love it', he admits. But it is true that there is an aim behind it all. If they write about Momy, they're also discussing Gibraltar – and, in 2012, they were talking of his feelings about the Rock's relationship to Britain and, above all, to the Queen, of whom it is easy to believe that he considers himself the world's largest fan.

Although he would never admit it, he would probably have preferred Her Majesty to have been dressed in red and white, the national colours of Gibraltar. It's not such a fantasy. Take a bright sunny day in late autumn 2012. In a year dominated by the Diamond Jubilee and the Olympics (in which, to his chagrin, his country was not allowed to compete), the place most people know as 'The Rock' was celebrating its national day. Almost everyone was in red and white. There was bunting in the streets and music playing in the square at the end of Main Street, and to describe the mood as festive would be like saying that the famed opening ceremony of those Olympics was an interesting event.

National Day? For those around him, it could have been Momy Day. As he walked – no, paraded would be a more accurate description – down Main Street, I counted forty people stopping to say 'hello' in the space of that parade in which he almost danced. They jostled for a place in front of him to show affection for the Momy who wore a red jacket, white trousers and a red-and-white hat, for the half-mile or so from his office to the main celebrations. They stopped him as he went – from the local bishop, to the chief justice, to the postman, to a tenant who had just rented a flat through his estate agency.

It isn't just a National Day phenomenon. It happens all the time. 'Yes, that's the trouble', says the man who would really feel he was in trouble if it didn't happen. 'I can't do anything wrong.' Rather, he wouldn't be allowed to *do* anything wrong. The trouble is that virtually the whole of the Rock's population would know if he committed the slightest offence. He only has to mention a local issue to a fellow citizen and the *Gibraltar Chronicle* newspaper or the country's TV station will ring him for an interview. He can usually find the time to do it. Try to stop him!

That really is part of the Rock's way of life: 'I can tell you that when I go down, now from nine o'clock in the morning till four o'clock in the afternoon, a lot of coaches come in from Spain filled with tourists. And yet I can point out who is a Gibraltarian and who is not.' How? His answer is perfectly obvious to him. 'We know each other', he explains.

Particularly the Jewish population. 'But not just the Jewish people. We are all one family.' Yet he agrees that 'as for the Jewish community, I know all of them.'

Momy was happy that day – although it has to be said that, even with the outfit he had created for the occasion, he wasn't, perhaps, at his sartorial best. This is a man described to me, by his successor as Mayor of Gibraltar, as 'our Beau Brummell' – never without not just a well-tailored suit, but a properly fashioned bow tie and a hat that is guaranteed to match the rest of the ensemble.

All that, however, is jumping our story a bit. It is important to point out once more, and right at the beginning, giving it due emphasis, that Momy was the first Mayor of Gibraltar – at least the first not to be a political appointment ('I vote for what is best for Gibraltar', he says).

A JP, a former officer in the Royal Gibraltar Regiment, the holder of an MBE, a leading light in the commercial affairs of his beloved Rock – that, it seems, is Momy. But actually that is not quite so. Let's go back to Momy (or, if we must be pedantic, National) Day. Before leaving to join the parade – or rather present his own – he is in his living room, in his red-and-white outfit, with the straps of *tefillin* wrapped around his left hand, one leather box containing verses from the Torah above his elbow, another box with other verses above his hairline, with two more straps hanging from it. Quietly, he is reciting morning prayers, as his forebears have done in Gibraltar now for centuries, and which he has done, without fail, since his barmitzvah at the age of 13. The *tefillin* and the red-and-white get-up jointly symbolize the man born Solomon Levy.

And if there were a crown to embroider on the little bag containing the phylacteries, he'd have it, too. But what if the wearer of that crown was called Charles? Would he still feel the same sense of loyalty if the Queen were no longer alive? 'No. He would automatically become king and I'd have to get used to it. Of course, seriously, I would respect Charles as king because he's the King of England. His office.'

He maintains that it's all a question of good manners: 'I believe we have to be grateful. If someone gives me something, I say "Thank you". Britain has looked after Gibraltar's interests, although at the moment they would love us to say we want to be Spanish.' That's the Foreign Office he's talking about:

> We are an embarrassment to them. They want to have a good relation with Spain. They say because of us, they can't have one. They wanted to give Spain 50 per cent sovereignty – but without our consent. They want to give half of the Rock away! Can you believe it? There's no oil in Gibraltar, so they don't care about us

> like they do about the Falklands. Malta's gone. Cyprus has gone – yet Gibraltar they still have. Don't forget we are the key to the Mediterranean.

If Momy is popular, which he is, he is so despite his profession. You wouldn't normally put estate agents at the top of the world's most respected and admired occupations. But he seems to be the exception confirming the general rule. As he told me: 'Estate agents have the reputation for being sharks. But thank God, in my case I am not a shark.' Besides which, shark is not a kosher breed of fish.

He is also the only auctioneer on the Rock, a business that hasn't exactly kept him busy. Only once in fifty-two years of operations has he conducted a property auction. He would like to think that if he fixes a price for a house or flat, no one sees any necessity to argue with him.

He is not just the most devoted and patriotic Gibraltarian one could imagine, but a leader of the Rock's Jewish community – only, according to some more optimistic assessments, about 800 people strong. But since there are only 30,000 people altogether living there, it is perhaps, per capita, the biggest Jewish congregation in the world outside of Israel, close to 3 per cent (American Jews represent about 1 per cent of their nation).

Actually, there is something of a dispute as to how many Jews there are on the Rock. The 800-odd figure comes from Momy's youngest brother, James Levy. Momy says the official figure is 650, of whom all but fifty are native-born Gibraltarians. It is plainly no easier to argue with James's brother Momy – even if the percentage of Jews is, according to the older brother, smaller. It would still represent the world's second biggest per capita community.

'It used to be 2,000 before the Second World War', says James. 'Then it went down to 550. Now we're about 800, without counting the Israelis. We think there are about 150 Israelis. Very few of them have anything to do with the community. They're just scared. It's their privilege. When they need us, we're there.'

There are those – or at least, there *were* those – native Jews in Gibraltar who were scared, too. Jews love proverbs, probably because they can relate to them all. The Rock seemed at one time to epitomize one of the most famous: the community that doesn't want to get rid of its rabbi is not a real community. The rabbi who agrees to go is not a real man ('mensch').

This is a place where once all wasn't as sunny as it now seems – when there is no cloud of a literal kind over the Rock, that is, a cloud that can block out the bright sunlight for hours.

'It was a terrible situation', James recalls. 'Brother didn't speak to brother.' (Not the Levy brothers, it has to be said.) 'It was awful. A rabbi we had was very charismatic. He left here to become a rabbi in Holland. He didn't like Holland and wanted to come back to Gibraltar. Half the community wanted him to come back and the other half didn't. I was chosen as the compromise candidate for president of the community then.'

At the time of the rows over the rabbi, he says, both sides wanted to run the community. 'So there was a mixed board, consisting of both sides with a compromise that he would be brought back and an educationalist would be brought in to run the schools, because neither wanted to run the education side. And, eventually, thank God, you know I think we got the community going again, but these were very difficult times, very difficult times. Thank God, we now have a peace – to the extent that I really would like to retire – but everyone's urging me to stay.'

That would be after two stints – the first lasted nine years. He is now in his thirteenth year of his second period of office. When he finishes his current term he will have been the longest-serving occupier of the office since the nineteenth century.

'I'd like to go but at the moment people think I should stay one more term, which is three years. I've lost a bit of my enthusiasm for it and therefore I think I should give it over to younger people.' If he is persuaded, it is because he is something of a no-nonsense peacemaker.

Momy himself has been spared those problems. He's a tall man, with a beard and a sleeked-back hairstyle that some might say typifies that Beau Brummell style. You have the feeling that he might welcome the return of powdered wigs, to say nothing of frills and tights, but he makes do with colourful waistcoats. And that, in a way, is a statement. His personality is a combination of establishment and individuality – a case of twin passions, his country and his religion. Or the other way around, depending on his mood, perhaps.

Amazingly – at least as far as people in the public eye in other countries might think – he has achieved his remarkable status in Gibraltar while, at the same time, observing Orthodox Jewish practice to the letter. He and his ever-expanding family (at the last count there were twenty-three grandchildren) not only observe the Sabbath and the Jewish Holydays with no exceptions, they keep the kashrut dietary laws to the optimum degree. Even when he did his National Service in what is now the Royal Gibraltar Regiment, Momy did the unheard-of thing: he told his officers what he could do, rather than the usual other way round. Having said that, we shall see that on every Christmas he was the only one in the barracks, holding the fort, as it were, while the other soldiers were at home or in church with their families. That, too, you could argue, sums him up.

So, I suppose, does his use of language – English most of the time, Spanish when dealing with some local Members of Parliament, Gibraltar's ministers, business men and women, and most of the people who stop him in the street – and not just on National Day. You can't sit in the open-air (kosher) restaurant run by one of his four daughters and move from one course to another without at least half a dozen people just wanting to talk or to wave.

He and his beloved wife, Sarah – who is, he says, even more religious than he is himself – tend to speak Spanish to each other, although she, too, is bilingual. It is, I suppose, another of those seeming contradictions in his life. 'English is my mother tongue', he maintains.

It is all tied up in that question of loyalties. Britain or Spain? Whether it's political or sporting – apart from one particular pastime: Spain would win hands down if it were merely a question of bullfighting, for this man breaks all the rules of political correctness, and most of the people who otherwise think that he is close to their ideal citizen love seeing a matador at work – there is no competition. Certainly, the question of language would never be allowed to be the main issue.

'We have a well-known saying, "British we are and we stay, but Spanish we speak all day." That's our Gibraltarians. That's our identity. Mind you, when I go to Spain, they think I'm a Spaniard. When I say I'm English, they think I'm joking. When I tell them I'm from Gibraltar, they keep quiet.'

His British loyalty, however, is never something to joke about. In fact, if the British media want a Gibraltarian view on their country's status, Momy is there in the foreground to fly the Union Jack, alongside Gibraltar's own red-and-white flag. You could sometimes say that he is more loyal than the people to whom he shows that loyalty: 'Prince Charles once came to Seville with Camilla on a visit, but he didn't come to Gibraltar because, had he come, the King of Spain wouldn't have liked it.' As it was, the Queen of Spain boycotted the banquet that Elizabeth II held for overseas royalties at the time of the Diamond Jubilee. The Queen won't come here because she does not want to upset her cousins in Madrid, Momy says:

> Unfortunately, the Foreign Office bowed down. They're damned scared. We are an impediment to them. They want life to be easy for them and we are making it difficult in the sense that we don't give way. If we were to say, 'You know, we want to become

> Spanish', they'd do something. But it's never going to happen. Prince Charles was greeted by the Spanish Crown Prince. He didn't mention Gibraltar, but he said, 'It's a pity we can never come to an agreement about our internal problem.'

That sort of thing infuriates anyone called Levy – at least, members of the Gibraltar branch. Momy sent a protest note to Whitehall:

> The Foreign Office wrote back to say that it doesn't stop royalty coming to Gibraltar (as they do to prevent members of the Royal Family going to Israel). In fact, they say that in 2009 Princess Anne and her husband came here to open a medical centre – and she's the Queen's daughter. So I wrote back to them, saying: 'I thank you for your letter, conscious that we can be carefully noted. I know Princess Anne came to Gibraltar in 2009 because I sat next to her having dinner in the Governor's residence. I was there because I was the Mayor. Also, I wrote letters of protest to the Spanish press saying that with all due respects to the heir to the throne, Gibraltar will never be Spanish. One [influential] Spaniard told me, 'We have enough problems of our own without having Gibraltar.' They have an expression: 'When you have a silver fish, it is a bone in the heart.' Well, that bone must have been taken to the heart by now after 300 years.'

It was those 300 years since the Treaty of Utrecht ceded the Rock to Britain.

No, it is going to stay British, Momy maintains, and this British outpost will never lose its Jewish flavour for people like him. 'It always reminds me of *Fiddler on the Roof* – you know, the way we dress, the food we eat ... it's exactly like that. Tradition!'

Tradition? Indeed, the devotion to it often appears to be Momy's main concern in life (his family apart). But he wouldn't like anyone to think that he lives in the nineteenth or any other century. The waistcoats, bow ties and bowler hats disguise a man with his feet firmly in the twenty-first.

Clothes are very important to him. Take him to London (but he doesn't need to be taken there; he goes frequently) and he will find a menswear outlet as if he were mentally equipped with a kind of satellite navigation device that takes him to the place where he'll find a suit, a pair of shoes or a collection of shirts that he will take home with him. His wife says she doesn't mind indulging him in the habit, by which he is convinced he would otherwise be considered either as one of yesterday's men or as a customer at some imaginary charity shop. If so, he thinks those people in Main Street would show sympathy for the fact that he has worn the same clothes twice in the past month. 'I went to Selfridges', he told me. 'I saw a beautiful jacket there. I tried it on. It looked very, very nice. I said, "I'll take it." He took it for £600. As he is likely to say, he can't take his money with him, but you are left with the distinct impression that he'd like to take his clothes (and all his toys, more about which later) along. And one thing leads to another: 'In London, I went to the Westfield shopping centre. I saw a blue suit that I thought I must have. So I bought it. Then I realized I had to have a hat to go with it.' No sooner thought than paid for.

It is perfectly true that if he were not dressed according to his own lights when he paraded down Main Street, people would talk. It would probably make the front page of the *Gibraltar Chronicle*. So while he looks good, all is well with him – and, you might like to add, with Gibraltar itself.

In fact, his whole family regard this as one of his most attractive characteristics. He likes his own definitions of fashion, partly, one might think because it identifies him as a man of the age, although not many men of his age look quite as chic as he does. His only son, Isaac Levy, says: 'He is a man of the present. I'm the one more interested in our history.' He will be the one who leaps to give dates in family history – of the distinguished ancestor, for example, who died in 1831. Isaac is the one who will present his biography of a near namesake, Moses de Isaac Levy, who revelled in the title 'Don'. That is another indication of the two worlds in which the family have lived. Moses was the founder of the family business, Levy & Co., which 'extended from shipping and trading in commodities such as timber, oil, coffee and sugar from Gibraltar'.

Levy & Co. is no longer in operation – at least, not in that form. Nevertheless, there is a distinct impression of a family business still functioning, the one you might be tempted to call simply 'Gibraltar'. Except it operates in very different ways and puts a great deal more into its operations than it takes out.

The story of the don – who would never have imagined his title could be shared by those gentlemen with broken noses known as the Mafia – is very much the story of the family as well as of the Jews of the Rock. They were descendants of Inquisition survivors; the term 'survivor' seems to have been reserved, in recent years, for those who survived the Holocaust, but the Inquisition was also, in its way, a calamity beyond imagination.

He and his family settled in Northern Morocco in the city of Tetuan, which appears to have been a town with 5,000 Jews, a large number of whom were in maritime trade. Although Moses was the first member of the family whose life was in any way documented, the contemporary Isaac is sure that the man's great-grandfather was a dayan (religious judge) named Yitzhak Halevy. He is the first family member whose name appears on Levy marriage certificates or *ketubat*. Also recorded is a street in the old Tetuan Jewish quarter named Calle Rabbi Yeshua Halevy (Yeshua was that Yitzhak's son).

Even before that, in 1708 a Jewish man called Hassan settled in Gibraltar. 'He became the postman', says Momy. 'He wasn't related to us.' That wasn't a flippant remark. Only a short talk with any member of the Levy clan reveals the fact that almost every Jew on the Rock has some familial connection. Besides which, Hassan is a very distinguished local moniker, and Momy's mother had that surname. But no one can see a connection with Hassan the postman. As we shall soon see, Hassan the Chief Minister, yes, but Hassan the postman, no.

The postman, however, would have to wait more than twenty years before he could deliver letters to other Jews, although he was officially working for the army. But then, in 1729, a rabbi named Yaakov Taurel left Morocco for Gibraltar, the place which the British had captured in 1704. From that date, supposedly, Jews started coming. Some seem to have been eighteenth-century commuters who constantly travelled to Africa and back. They appear to have been encouraged to become traders working with the British forces, rather like the chandlers who settled in places such as Portsmouth and Plymouth, thus founding some of England's earliest communities. Don Moses was among these, although he refused to go undercover, as the British admiral who took them from Gibraltar to Lisbon recommended. The Inquisition's ban on Jews entering Portugal was still in force. It turned out, however, that the prospect of trade overran any influence of the anti-Semitism engendered by the Church.

It also overran the Treaty of Utrecht, which, like so many other international documents, has in its Article 10 that no Jews would be allowed to live on the Rock. So when they first went there, no one was supposed to know about it.

But they continued to make their mark – in Britain as well as in Gibraltar. A visit to Moses at the Anglo-Jewish Association in 1877 by his grandson, Solomon de J. Levy, and his great-grandson Abraham, is recorded in the family archives.

So, plainly, the idea of Jews in Gibraltar is far from a new phenomenon. In the 1720s, they established what is today the oldest synagogue in the city, the Shaar Hashemaim (the Gates of Heaven) as well as a yeshiva (Talmudical college), the Etz Haim, a name used for schools of the kind all over the world. So a Jewish community set itself up, probably without realizing what it was doing. It certainly didn't consider it was establishing the Levy dynasty in what could be considered to be the least likely location. When a great-great-great- (Momy can no longer work out exactly how many 'greats' there were) grandfather settled on the Rock, he registered his residency there: 'As a result, 250 years ago, we all became Gibraltarians.'

Meanwhile, they started trading with other countries, with the help of the British, who doubtless saw this as an expansion of their own nation's influences.

All this is music to Momy's son's ears. The twenty-first-century Isaac will admit – his father readily confirms it – that he is even more religious than Momy is himself, which may seem strange to those not used to people who pray three times a day (with *tefillin* in the morning), and eating only kosher food (to the point that Momy is close to despair during the nine days in the summer when even meat that satisfies all the dietary laws is forbidden – the reasons are too obtuse to go into here). About his own religious upbringing, Isaac says: 'It was very much laissez-faire. Nothing was ever stuffed down my throat. That attitude made me want to do it for myself.'

To Momy himself, religion – tradition again – and history are closely entwined. Which has a great deal to do with the fact that he alone could support the kosher meat industry, or certainly that which reaches the Rock of Gibraltar. Seeing Momy in his suit, tie and waistcoat, doing what he believes should be done to a leg of lamb, is a sight indeed to behold. He is also a wine connoisseur. A kosher wine connoisseur, which is a breed not universally known. In fact, he will tell with glee about the time that he ate at a kosher hotel and asked for a bottle of wine. He noticed that the entire dining room was silent.

Almost all the tables were occupied by people staring at him. It was like a Bateman cartoon – I could see the caption as he told me the story: 'The man who asked for a bottle of kosher wine.' There is one shop where the orders are taken for kosher food from London, which is then flown in to the new Gibraltar International Airport. 'That shop has everything. And the best thing is he has the best selection of kosher wine anywhere. Beautiful!'

You have to understand that Momy Levy is a one-man public relations operation on behalf of not just the Rock's Jewish community, but of the Rock itself, which he loves so much. He doesn't always want to talk about himself – and this is a man who had stamps printed with his portrait on them; not real postage stamps, but ones which are called, in the world of philately, 'labels'. They look like stamps and go alongside real Gibraltar stamps on the letters he sends. One of the 'labels' shows him with a group of local clergymen, the bishop, the rabbi and other dignitaries, all shaking hands. That is as much a tribute to the need for good interfaith relations as anything else. And you can forgive the fake stamps. To him, it's just one of his toys. But good relations between the faiths is part of Momy's very being.

The local rabbi, Ronnie Hassid, talked to me about the time that the then Chief Minister, Joe Bossano, once said how glad he was that the Jewish community was so well tolerated in Gibraltar. The rabbi took umbrage:

> I said that to tolerate may be something you show for people from outside. Like tolerate the tall people or the short people. I mean we're all Gibraltarians. When the Chief Rabbi of France came here he said how nice it was that we were so well tolerated and that it's so nice that there is peace between us all, I said, 'Look you may tolerate somebody who is obnoxious. But our Jewish people are not obnoxious. We are nice people, part of Gibraltar.'

And Gibraltar's Jews have stopped tolerating a lot too, says the rabbi:

> There used to be a lot of intermarriage, perhaps 70 or 80 per cent. People would go to Morocco and have quickie conversions. Thanks to Momy's father and others, we stopped that. Now conversions have to be done with the authority of the Gibraltar community. It's a difficult conversion and highly respected internationally. Now marrying out is not on anyone's agenda. You will not find anyone under the age of 40 whom would dream of marrying [out].

There is another point that the rabbi who teaches at the Hebrew school, the Talmud Torah, believes should be emphasized. With the increase in orthodoxy, there is a risk that parents will frown on the idea of a secular education, which is why some go to London and Israel to have a religious schooling. 'There is competition to be *frummer* (more religious) than the Joneses [or the Cohens] next door. There's a lot of peer pressure there to be *frummer* than the next guy. But the boys [can be] streetwise, but they don't know the rules of their own game necessarily. Of course, I highly value a secular education.'

Momy, with his own history behind him, says 'Hear! hear!' to that and certainly to the idea of interfaith relations. It is a story to be told whenever Momy is guest of honour at some Gibraltar banquet or other – and there are always a lot of those occasions, when he is guest of honour and when this story is told. It is one story among many that His Excellency the Governor loves to tell about his friend Mr Levy.

He knows that we know he loves being in the public eye, and Gibraltar benefits from this man who prefaces almost every statement he makes about himself with the words 'Modesty apart' – but since both Gibraltar and Judaism are so entwined in his very existence, and since the history of both seems so often to be almost part of his own family story, any modesty would be out of place.

At the drop of one of those bowlers, he will tell you about Aaron Cardoso, who was a friend of Horatio Nelson. 'Nelson told him before Trafalgar: "If I survive this, I'll get you out of this black hole". The black hole was Gibraltar. He called it "this dark piece of the world". I've never forgiven him for that. But he was interesting. I am told that in the mid-nineteenth century, he applied to Spain to live there because he suffered from asthma.'

It was all due, Cardoso believed, to that big cloud around the Rock, which is not considered an advantage to those afflicted by the condition. The Spanish Inquisition wasn't much help to him either. They refused to allow the man to settle in their country. If they had, being placed in front of the men in hoods who stood before the big cross might have had an even more serious effect on his breathing.

But that was a long time ago. Momy is much more concerned by the people who don't say nasty, unpleasant things about Gibraltar, but are not, he is sure, as friendly as they ought to be.

Ask the Governor, who revels in the number of Solomon Levy (occasionally, for the sake of variety, it is useful to remind people of his real full name) anecdotes and he'll happily find one for the right occasion:

> He told me a lovely story about his conversation with a Barcelona taxi driver, who asked where he was from. When Momy told him, the taxi driver exclaimed, 'Gibraltar Espanol!' Momy asked the driver if he was a good Roman Catholic. 'Of course', replied the driver. 'Well', said Momy, 'your messiah came 2,000 years ago, but I am Jewish and mine has not arrived yet. But when he does, Gibraltar will still be British.' Apparently, he and the driver parted friends.

Momy maintains that he doesn't let things like that bother him too much – 'my philosophy in life is to be happy with what I have got. I want happiness and good health and for my family to have good health. I want to be peaceful here, to have good health, to enjoy the life I only live once and that is my motto in life. And, of course, not to do harm to anybody.'

The Governor says a hearty 'Hear! hear!' to that. Also, he enjoys putting things into a spiritual context when it comes to Momy, a man he is pleased to note is a 'huge supporter of interfaith friendships and we often see him in the cathedral for services. We saw him there for the Diamond Jubilee choral evensong. After the service, he said he had to dash away to the synagogue, saying with a twinkle in his eye that he was hedging his bets and covering all bases just in case.'

Ask any member of the family whom they look to as the founder of the dynasty of communal workers and they will speak of their uncle Joshua, Sir Joshua Hassan, the first mayor and then Chief Minister of Gibraltar, a man who, Momy says, was very much a favourite of the Queen, who loved his obvious devotion to Britain and his unwavering determination never to sell out to Spain.

That, of course, ticks all the right boxes, as the contemporary cliché goes. Certainly, it does for Momy and his youngest brother James.

Momy's other brother – younger than he, older by twelve years than James – is Rabbi Abraham Levy, the retired spiritual head of Britain's Spanish and Portuguese congregation. He is not quite as enthusiastic about Gibraltar's British links as are his siblings. 'Yes, that is quite true. I would be more in favour of a compromise situation than they would.'

That doesn't mean that this Levy is less devoted to the land of his fathers. While his roots may be embedded in the less rocky parts of the Gibraltar school, Abraham is the brother who has spent the least time there – which, speaking with the tongue firmly in the cheek, plainly was not the reason he was awarded his Spanish knighthood, the first Gibraltarian to be given the honour (subsequently, another member of the Rock's community, Sol Seruya, was also knighted by Spain's king). Abraham went to school in Britain and then studied at Jews' College in London. So, he says, he spent barely six years in what for his brothers is, in every conceivable way, home.

'I am, though', he told me, 'very proud of the history that we have in Gibraltar. And the influence has been there all my life. I think like a Gibraltarian.' And like a Jew so connected with Spanish history. Abraham raised an interesting point:

> the Jews remained away from Spain for hundreds of years [after the Inquisition], whereas they started to go back to Germany less than twenty years after [the] Holocaust. Nevertheless, the pride they had in having been in Spain was such that they kept their language. They are still proud of it. My own father-in-law was overheard one day speaking a language that seemed very strange to a man who couldn't understand how he could be talking in a form of Spanish that went out centuries earlier. What my father-in-law was speaking, he explained, was Ladino, a Jewish form of Spanish which very few still speak today.

There are also those, Rabbi Levy points out, who still carry the keys to houses they were forced to leave in the fifteenth century in the hope they would one day go back, which seems to display a great deal of faith, not only in eventual justice, but also in the quality of pre-1492 building standards. 'I have had people come to me who have established a community in a town in Portugal after returning to Judaism. They've opened a synagogue there and restarted everything needed for a Jewish community.' He said that is happening constantly:

> I had someone come to see me in my office from Mallorca. He said, 'I'm a Jew, rabbi.' I said 'How do you know?' He said, 'Because we have some traditions.' And he gave me one. He said,

> 'My parents always bought a side of ham and I've always bought one. Never to eat it, but to hang it at the front window so that people who pass by thought we were eating it and we wouldn't be accused of being crypto Jews.'

If that sort of story is constantly recurring – and it is – it is not a tale demonstrated in Gibraltar.

The people who arrived on the Rock after the first years of the Treaty of Utrecht came, as much as anything, because they knew they could establish a community that kept to its traditions and standards without a need to look over their shoulders. Although it has a reputation now for increasing orthodoxy, Rabbi Levy would like to think of it as like his own former fiefdom in London, a Judaism, as he says, without adjectives.

That seems to be one of the secrets for the success of the Jewish community on the Rock. As for Sir Joshua himself, he is still the pride and joy of the Jewish community, years after his death. He was a regular congregant at one of Gibraltar's four synagogues. Yes, four, all in use on Shabbat, the Jewish Sabbath, and each taking it in turns to hold services on weekdays: services that are – uniquely, perhaps, for a small community – filling the buildings virtually to capacity. Go into the one currently being used on an ordinary Monday evening, perhaps, and it will seem like a High Holyday in a British provincial town's place of worship. The mornings are even more remarkable. As Momy put it: 'We have three morning services. We have one at about 7 o'clock for the *frummers* (the most religious) which has about fifteen worshippers, another at half past seven for the workers, which attracts eighteen men, and the most popular, a third for the rich, at half past eight, to which fifteen men go.' There are ten ordained rabbis in Gibraltar, who are members of the *kollel* – but one communal rabbi who teaches and produces a weekly religious tract which he posts through the doors of his congregants' houses, never missing out one of them. Services are conducted by either these reverend gentlemen or learned laymen – and there are a lot of those.

This enthusiasm for prayer has a lot to do with the influx of new religious blood into Gibraltar: 'What happens is that young men go to England to university, they meet girls in London who are Ashkenazi and very religious, bless them.' His very use of that term indicates a degree of religiosity in himself, of course. 'They come back here and they want to establish themselves – but adopting the Ashkenazi *frum* ways. Yes, it's very, very unusual in an essentially Sephardi community.'

The men who pray – or daven, as their Ashkenazi Orthodox brothers would call it – don't depend on going to the synagogue to keep up with their Torah study. They are the 'students' at the *kollel,* a small religious college. Religious life is clearly even more intense than it was when Sir Joshua Hassan was the leading citizen on the Rock. According to Momy's son, Isaac Levy, the former Chief Minister is a source of a great deal of pride to his nephew: 'He was very proud when Joshua received his knighthood.' The extent to which that pride manifested itself will become obvious in a later chapter.

Sarah and Momy have made sure that the link between country and religion continues. Their five children – most of whom married English-speakers – have no problem with either tongue. Inevitably, with such a large family of high achievers, the clan is split geographically. Their son and two of their four daughters are living in London.

If language dictates culture, then you can say that the Levy family are almost (and I say 'almost' advisedly) as British as they are Jewish. But not quite. On the other hand, Sunday morning would be a rather different occasion if there weren't the BBC political programmes to which Momy – sitting without his jacket and, in summer, in shorts (nobody outside the family or his intimate friendships could imagine it) – is totally addicted. He has to see BBC2's *Newsnight* programme before he goes to bed. It's as though it's a declaration of loyalty, if not patriotism.

Friends have to hope that when he is watching TV, some producer not caring too much about what happens in faraway Gibraltar doesn't get it into his head to play the National Anthem. The moment the opening chords of 'God Save the Queen' are struck, Momy will jump out of his armchair and stand to attention. 'Sorry', he says in explanation. 'I can't sit while the National Anthem is being played.' He has, it hardly needs to be said, almost the same reverence for the English language. 'I tell you', he says, 'if the phone rings now, I speak English first.'

Perhaps it's being Jewish, perhaps it's just what living in Gibraltar does: linguistically, the Levy family present something of an anomaly. Momy's wife, as you might expect from a woman who worked in London for a fair amount of time, speaks fluent English. 'But Sarah and I never speak English to each other. But now I have to speak in English to my grandchildren because they don't know Spanish, unfortunately. So we also speak Llanito – which, just as Yiddish could be called rotten German, is a mixture. It is Gibraltar's own language, half English, half Spanish.' He even speaks the dialect without realizing it. 'When I don't remember an English word, I say it in Spanish – and vice versa.'

History has had its impact on language, too. And on culture. Momy says that to his intense disappointment, his son Isaac has one considerable flaw in his development: 'At the age of 8, I was taken to a bullfight and loved it. Now, Isaac doesn't know a thing about bullfighting.' He says it the way a father with a season ticket to Arsenal or Manchester United might decry a son's lack of interest, let alone enthusiasm for the British national game.

Momy can't understand why his adoration of the bullring should be frowned upon by so many people. Fortunately, the Royal Society for the Prevention of Cruelty to Animals, the RSPCA, haven't spoken to him about it – even though they did manage to get the activity banned in Gibraltar itself. 'I must say, with all due respect to the RSPCA, I do love bullfighting.' It is not such a problem for him, all things considered. If he fancies a bit of four-legged blood and gore, all he has to do is walk across the frontier to La Linea, which might take him as long as fifteen minutes. Such is life in a place like Gibraltar, where General Franco closed the border for seventeen years. (He always says, as we shall note, that Franco was his marriage broker. Because of the frontier ban, he had to think seriously about marrying a local girl. There were other reasons they married, but Sarah doesn't appear to show any resentment when he tells the story often, as he does with most of his best anecdotes.)

The Levys come, as we shall also see, from a religious family with numerous famous rabbis in its line. They are people who, in their own way, helped to build up the very unusual Jewish community that is Gibraltar Jewry.

The grandchildren go to the Talmud Torah in the centre of town. Well, of course they do. And that is where you get to see the roots of this remarkable Jewish community, which are extended with the private high schools that have been established, one for girls, one for boys. The government provided the premises, on a long lease.

Momy's two brothers are both, in their way, communal leaders, although one of them achieved fame outside. As we have seen, Rabbi Abraham Levy, Momy's closest sibling, has just retired as the spiritual leader of the Spanish and Portuguese congregation in Britain. His youngest brother, James (or Haim, as Momy calls him) is to the Jews of the Rock what Momy is to the general community – although that is an unfair limitation to all that he does. He heads the biggest law firm in Gibraltar and can spend a week in half-a-dozen different countries. He is very much a power in local – which of course means national – politics. He has more than once been touted as a coming Chief Minister, but he is probably too busy dealing with other things and spending an hour on religious study every morning before going to the synagogue.

'I'm very Orthodox', says James, who thinks that if he ever retired from his legal 'business', it would give him more time to study 'and to get involved in more social projects, rather than just running the community'.

They are extraordinarily close, these two brothers – except not everyone thinks they *are* brothers. As Momy told me: 'A lot of people think he is my nephew. I still have people ask me, "How's your nephew?" They really think I am his uncle.' If so, a very proud uncle at that.

Momy goes on, singing his brother's praises, which is perhaps his own way of saying *tehillim*, 'I have to say that while I am watching the Parliament channel on BBC television, he is studying or doing some good work somewhere.' Such praise is more usually heard for an elder brother than a younger one.

'Just running the community' is something of an oxymoron. James agrees that he is 'very committed' and, on the very day we met at his office, he had spent most of the morning dealing with 'a very sensitive issue'. As he said: 'I think we've got the right answer, but I don't know. We never know.' For a lawyer, that is indeed a problem.

To add to their family's Orthodox credentials, both their sisters, Nita – who lives in Milwaukee – and Loli, in London, are married to rabbis. Momy likes to talk about the time that Nita married her American rabbi husband:

> They took the ship to America five days after their wedding. They took all their presents with them. When they arrived, they started to take all their things out and began to worry about the duty to be paid. The customs man saw all these brand-new things and

> asked, 'What's going on here?' They told him they were wedding presents. He said he was going to give them a present, too – not charge them any duty.

Could that, too, be part of the Levy family magic?

Two of Momy's daughters, Kelly and Ruth, who have stayed in Gibraltar, are also married to rabbis. So is Bathsheba (known as Babsy), who lives in London, along with their other sister, Giselle – who breaks the trend by being the wife of a TV producer. Their sole brother, Isaac, is a lawyer-cum-businessman, who, in the Sephardi tradition, has called his own son Solomon. In fact, among Sarah and Momy's twenty-three grandchildren, there are altogether five Solomons (the Askanazi, or East and mid-European, Jewish practice is not to name children after living relatives).

I often wonder – and, of course, I'm not alone in this – if people living in what some might conclude is something of a golden age, are also dwelling in a kind of fool's paradise. Momy riles at the idea: not at the use of the word 'fool' – which he manifestly is not – but at the notion behind the phrase:

> Never. Not at all. This is my home. We all live naturally. Nothing, no put-ons, no hiding. We could move out – but we won't. It has always been like that for us. And it doesn't help. I mean, God forgive me, my wife is much more *frum* than I am. I'm 76, and since I was 22 I haven't changed. I mean, I've changed in the sense that I don't drink (except wine) and I have had to give up cigars for medical reasons. But otherwise, I am the same. I suppose, I know I'm wrong. After all, we live in a community. We're all one big family and we mustn't stand out.

That, of course, is not the only reason: 'It's such a small place, it's easy to be religious.'

This tiny country is just that: a country, if one in miniature. It not only has its own prime minister (the title Momy likes to give to the Chief Minister), its parliament and its own supreme court (of which the Jewish former British solicitor and county court judge Barrington Black was appointed a justice at the age of 80 in 2012) and its own army; every international bank you could think of has a branch there, as does every insurance company.

The shops in Main Street include – well, they would, wouldn't they? – Marks & Spencer. There is also a Morrisons supermarket. What is different about commercial life is the number of boutiques and small shops that are not part of an international group. But, more significantly, a great many of them bear that sign of Jewish residence or business on their doorways, the *mazuza* – a metal tube containing the words of the religion's *cri de coeur*, the *Shema*, beginning with the words, 'Listen, O Israel, the Lord our God, the Lord is one.' For this is another indication of the sort of community it is. A walk down Main Street on a Saturday morning could deceive visitors into thinking this is a very sleepy little place. They won't have heard that Orthodox Jews close their businesses on a Sabbath – more proof that this is essentially a very Orthodox place.

It is very rare to see a Jewish shop open on Shabbat. Momy says: 'If there are Holydays on Thursday and Friday, then the shops are shut from Wednesday till the following Monday. There used to be one that did open, a bookshop, but that's been sold now. But otherwise never ever. Some of the shops would like to open but don't out of respect to the others.'

That, too, is good business practice, by men who regard business as part of their very existence. 'But the women, on the whole, don't work. Their work is looking after the children, the way it should be.' Momy, never shy about showing his true colours, was displaying them from his own flagpole or soapbox. Just as he does about his British links. As the Governor put it: ‘He is passionately British and passionately Gibraltarian. He genuinely believes that there’s no better place in the world than Gibraltar. And I believe that he has done a tremendous amount to bring together people of different faiths in Gibraltar, recognizing that this is his task.’

Momy’s own ‘spin’ on this is to put his loyalty in the context of a person showing gratitude for a gift:

> I’m now 76 years old and since the time I was born, they [the British] have looked after Gibraltar’s interests, which are my interests, and we have to be grateful for that. They used to be responsible for 100 per cent of our interests and gave us the money we needed. As time went on, we became more ... not independent ... but we became more self-contained. Even so, they have always looked after us and we are educated to be grateful. I have to say that even if I had been a Spaniard and the Spanish looked after us, I would also have been grateful.

To him, that is not only a Gibraltarian trait, it is part of a family tradition and very much part of Jewish teaching. After all, it is in British synagogues, not in churches, that prayers are read each week for the royal family. It was Jeremiah who taught that Jews had to ‘pray for the welfare of the city’. For city, read state; for state, in the Levys’ case, read Gibraltar.

Every Jew on the Rock feels the Momy way about the link with Britain. *Almost* every citizen, of whatever faith, thinks that too, he says: ‘Everybody, except one or two, would like to see a solution that once and for all ends the speculation.’ Not that he sees much speculation in yet another referendum, which he is certain would be a mere run-on from the previous voting exercise in 2004. ‘Except for one or two, everyone thinks the way I do’, he maintains. ‘There was a referendum in 1969. There were 12,550 people in favour of staying British and forty-four against. There, seriously, wouldn't be anything like forty-four who would oppose it today.'

Momy's friend, Danny Anthony Feetham, who is not only a partner of James Levy, but also the Leader of the Opposition, sees two things about Momy: his religious tolerance and his love of Britishness. 'Momy and I have been close for many, many years and he's always like an older brother for me. He's Jewish and I'm Catholic but we are very close.' On Momy's birthday, Danny Feetham presented him with an antique German-made silver Torah cover, which he saw in an antique shop in Toledo. He is confident that the link between the two crowns, the one that represents Judaism, the other Momy's beloved Queen, says it all: 'To me, he's just Mr British personified. Momy is the embodiment of everything that is British and everything that it is to be a British Gibraltarian.' Also, 'You know he is associated with defending the Queen, of promoting anything that is [to do with the] Royal Family in Gibraltar, that Britishness of which Momy is so much a part', he says. 'If you take the Britishness out of Gibraltarians there is something missing. There would certainly be something missing in Momy.'

If only he could persuade Britain not even to tinker with the way Gibraltar runs its affairs, he would be very happy indeed. He is gratified that the 'mother country' says that the people of the Rock should look after their own destiny, but he isn't totally comforted by the thought that they really mean it. 'What have they got to lose?' Momy asks: 'We are not a colony. We are *with* Britain, not *under* Britain. We are self-contained, we are self-sufficient. Britain does pay for the police and the Royal Gibraltar Regiment is part of the British Army. We always look after our financial affairs and we know how we react to foreign policy.' But he ploughs on: 'Economically, we don't take a penny from Britain. We used to, but we don't now. And Britain has the advantage of having a base here without having to pay for it.'

Momy told me he gives a lot of credit for the good relationship with Britain to the former Chief Minister:

> He established what became known as the Cordoba Agreement because it was at Cordoba that Spain and Britain made an agreement of sorts – not settling what was called the 'Gibraltar Question', but an agreement that no discussions between the two countries about us should be held without Gibraltar being represented.
>
> Sir Geoffrey Howe, who was Foreign Secretary at the time, would send him out of the room when there were talks with the Spanish Foreign Minister and then tell him afterwards, 'Hassan, we've decided this ... we've decided that ...'. But a few years ago, Moratinos, the Spanish Foreign Minister, and the then British Foreign Secretary, David Miliband, and our Chief Minister met together on equal terms. Miliband said that 'unless there's Gibraltar there, we will not talk'. So we achieved that.

There are other colours that Momy nails to his mast. While Gibraltar will stay British, he says – 'speaking as an idealist' – that he is convinced that one day Britain will be part of a united Europe. But until that day comes, Momy Levy, for one, says 'Hands off.' If they had their ears turned in the direction of Gibraltar – one almost thinks that a radio would have been superfluous, the Gibraltarians were shouting so loudly – the then British Government might have noted that their suggestion of shared 'ownership' of the Rock was being treated like the sound of guns trained on a Spanish warship in the Straits.

Strangely, for people who are not intimately involved in the life of Gibraltar, this small area which proclaims loyalty to the Crown and the British way of life has no representatives in Westminster. No MP for Gibraltar Central or anywhere else on the Rock. Momy remembers the way locals fought for inclusion in the British parliament. To some, it was a sort of declaration of just how British they felt: 'There was a very strong organization, the Pro-Integration Movement. They were fighting for it until Roy Hattersley, who was the minister then, said, "Integration, under no way."'

It was a slogan that Momy adopted himself, if not in so many words. 'I was completely against it because at the moment, we have 630 Members of Parliament. If something went wrong, I always felt that they would *all* fight for us, not just one local MP.' There are still people who follow the integration cause. 'I must say that when we have a problem, I write to individual MPs who always reply, ask sensible questions. I have had cases where I've had four MPs on the same afternoon asking questions about Gibraltar.' That is good and useful. On the other hand, there are no embassies in Gibraltar. For the most part, ambassadors to the Court of St James's have to look after their country's interests in Gibraltar, too. We have, in London, a large building where Mr Albert Poggio OBE and staff look after the affairs of Gibraltar very efficiently. For example, they are in constant touch with Members of Parliament, and they achieve very good results with their first class public relations.

United Europe:

> Yes, I'd like to see it. If that happens, of course, the word 'sovereignty' disappears and Spain can say once and for all, it doesn't matter to them. They can say, 'We don't want Gibraltar. We have enough problems of our own.' After all, it was only when Franco was there that Gibraltar was really important to them, when they used it as a means of diverting attention from Spain's other problems. The people of Spain don't even think about Gibraltar. And we give jobs to around 7,000 Spaniards here who were unemployed in their own country. So really they should be grateful to us, with the present large unemployment in the 'Campo' area (Gibraltar's vicinity).

The professions have their full quotas of Jewish practitioners: 'We have a few accountants, some lawyers, we have one dentist. It's a homely life here.'

Orthodoxy, Gibraltar style (which is in some cases also Stamford Hill or Borough Park style) is, he believes, practised by as many as 90 per cent of local Jews: 'There are just a few who don't keep kosher. But I'd say 95 per cent do.'

Somehow there is nothing incongruous about it. Maybe it's part of the Latin temperament, one that dictates that you accept the way of life chosen by others without turning a hair – or a conversation, the principal rule of which is to follow etiquette, particularly the part that says you don't interrupt other people when they are talking. To which, in Gibraltar, you can add that you take for granted the fact that what you say could easily be misconstrued. Take this for an example: you are continuing that walk down Main Street and you meet a friend. Say 'Hello'? No. They'll greet you with 'Goodbye'. Momy has an explanation for this strange turn of phrase, which some people would wish was really turned around: 'Sometimes, English people come here and they say, "Aren't they rude? They see me, but won't talk to me." In a way, it's a way of saying "Hello" – and "Goodbye" together. Like "Shalom" in Israel.'

It could possibly be interpreted, too, as a special kind of what the Marx Brothers called monkey business. There's the famous Rock Hotel at the bottom of what looks like the biggest stone in the world, and then the winding road to the top with the occasional building, mainly military outposts, and then there are the apes. You don't actually have to go to the summit to see or greet the apes, which look more like monkeys. They are just as likely to see and greet *you*. For they don't stay on top all the time. Every now and again, a warning goes out to close windows in case of a simian invasion. But then, Winston Churchill once declared that as long as there are apes in

Gibraltar, the territory will stay British. Of course, he hadn't met Momy Levy.

Not that everything is always bright and sunny. As we have seen, there are days when the place is shrouded by a mist that lingers a little too long around the rock, the famous 'cloud', the one shielding most of the area from the sun and making it seem unseasonably cold – which is not a word heard much in these parts. Certainly not among the Jews, who really do seem to think they are living in some kind of golden age, which is always a dangerous thought to have.

Momy will say that the reason for that is that the Jews, like their Gentile neighbours, have the welfare of the Rock so much at heart. As he said, 'Here in Gibraltar, there are socialists, Liberals, Conservatives. Momy votes for whatever is best for Gibraltar.' When he slips into the third person, as if he were discussing a figure from history – or contemporary politics, for that matter – you know he has a serious thought beneath that bowler hat of his. The hat – or at least that one – has quite a significance in the life of Momy Levy. Yes, it is easy to establish that he enjoys the Beau Brummell association, just as he enjoys being well dressed himself. But for him it is also a badge of honour and stands for something. It stands for his walks to and from the synagogue on Shabbat or the Holydays. It is almost as if it were a sign of piety, a kind of prayer – because by looking good he is showing his own idea of respect.

The hat also comes out on one particular occasion he wouldn't allow himself to miss – the first Sunday after Remembrance Day in London when he proudly marches past the Cenotaph in Whitehall, the sole member of the 'contingent' bearing the sign 'Gibraltar'. It is the annual service and parade organized by the Association of Jewish Ex-Servicemen and Women, a unique Anglo-Jewish (or, rather, British Jewish) occasion on which war veterans and the slightly younger ones, like Momy himself, who did their National Service, say a series of prayers, including the solemn Kaddish, in memory of those who fell in Britain's wars.

There was a time when even Momy did without the bowler at that unique ceremony of dedication. But that was when he was officially still in the Royal Gibraltar Regiment and went in uniform, a smart blue ensemble. I suspect he enjoys the Savile Row touch more, even if he is fortunate enough to be able to buy his clothes off the peg. Not that you would know it.

Momy has augmented his associations with fellow ex-servicemen by being at the very fulcrum of the Gibraltar branch of the Royal British Legion. Obviously – how could anything else have happened? – he became president of the branch for a while. However:

> There was another member, who was a lot older than I, and I said to him, 'Look, in the next election, I'm going to stand as chairman and you will stand as president – because you should be president.' So for the past twenty-six years I have been chairman. It is very rewarding. I have brought to Gibraltar three wounded soldiers who fought in Afghanistan. I organized for them to go down Main Street and I spoke to all the shopkeepers, asking for them to give them presents. Then the commander of the British forces here organized a tour around the Rock and they were given a chance to go in the sea – including one without legs. The only thing he had to say was 'Sir, it's rather cold in the water.'

He wouldn't regard that as charity, although the expression 'charity begins at home' is brought to mind. Soldiers from Britain are one thing. Entertaining local (non-Jewish) children is almost another. Almost, because he takes them for walks, too:

> I need to show that we are all part of Gibraltar, so every summer I take groups of children from every single school in Gibraltar

> around the synagogue. In a way, it is sad, because when I say, 'This is where Sir Joshua Hassan used to worship and this is where he sat', the 18-year-olds who come say 'Who was Sir Joshua Hassan?' That is about a man who served Gibraltar for forty years. So I took it to the Ministry of Education. They told me, 'Look Momy, we have so much about English history for GCSE.' I say, 'Incorporate it. We must know our own history.' It doesn't appear to have done much good.

That, too, is one of the reasons he tries so hard to work for good relationships in his tiny slice of the world. It certainly explains his need to look after the welfare of ex-servicemen. For him that is more than a duty, much more than merely a job that he believes he has to do. It is, in its way, a calling. It is as though he feels he has been especially called to perform a task, and failing to do so will have results he doesn't like to talk or even think about. Fortunately for him, others believe that about him, too. It means that when he needs something done, done it usually is.

His chairmanship of the Legion ranks with his presidency of the Jewish community and the time he became mayor – well, actually, nothing quite ranks with that in his mind – as the milestones in his life.

He won't say so, but much of what he does has only positive effects on the community over which he once presided. How many of the growing number of Orthodox Jewish citizens of Gibraltar actually know all that is perhaps a different matter, but they all benefit from it, without doubt.

Promenade through that same Main Street, midweek, and you might think you have been transported to the ultra-Orthodox area of Meir Sherim in Jerusalem. Women in headscarves push prams and what the Americans call 'strollers' to and from the main Jewish school (there is also a private nursery). Men in biggish black hats hustle by on their way to one of the four synagogues on the Rock – the Nefusot Yehuda (which is known as the 'Flemish Synagogue', because it is said to have been furnished in what is regarded as a particular Flemish style). Momy describes that as 'my mother's synagogue', the one that was used by the Hassan family. Then there is the 286-year-old Shaar Hashamayim, which is the biggest as well as the oldest; the Abudarham, which traditionally was the synagogue of the Levy family – 'when she married, my mother transferred to that one, like a footballer'. It's the one of which Momy is president today, and has been for thirty-six years. The fourth synagogue is the Etz Haim – for services early in the morning or in the afternoons or evenings. Add to that the services at the Talmud Torah school on Shabbat only, and you have five synagogues in Gibraltar.

Five synagogues for what could be a community of only 650 people (depending on which Levy brother you listen to) sounds a little extravagant. But Momy says:

> You tell a member of one of the synagogues that it might be a good idea to close his shul and use one of the others and he'll tell you where to get off. We want shalom in Gibraltar. We've always wanted peace. So we came to an agreement. We keep all four shuls – but use only one of them on week days, when they take it in turns, rotating them every three months. But on Shabbat and festivals we use them all.

The services in the synagogues are a little difficult for visitors from Britain or America to follow. Unless, that is, they are members of Abraham Levy's Spanish and Portuguese congregation. For these all follow the Sephardi ritual, which, in their case, owes more to the practices of the Jews of nearby Morocco than either Spain or Portugal. To complicate matters, the prayer books are in Hebrew – and Spanish, which gives a nice colourful touch to the ritual.

The community's rabbi – paid rabbi, that is; there are others – is British, with a Cambridge degree in engineering.

Sephardi and slightly obscure it might all feel, but Jewish education doesn't end with the Jewish schools. The *kollel* is certainly flourishing as a sort of mini yeshiva where young men train for the rabbinate and get a stipend to go along with their studies. The advantages that the local community can offer far outweigh those offered in their home countries. James Levy regards that as part of the attraction to Jews in Gibraltar – a country where, unlike most provincial outposts of Judaism in Britain, say, young people from abroad tend to come and stay, and locals leave for university and then return home.

The kosher shops appear to do a roaring trade and so do the three kosher restaurants – one of which is run by the local Jewish baker, who happens to be one of Momy's two daughters living in Gibraltar (another two are in London). Her bakery provides the only locally produced bread available on the Rock – other shops sell foods, including bread, from abroad either from Spain or flown in from Britain to the Morrisons supermarket and other local stores in Gibraltar.

Milk is flown in from England. That is also part of Momy's history:

> When I first came here after being educated and finishing my job as an estate agent in England, I used to go to the Rock Hotel and sit by the pool there. I used to meet British European Airways [now part of BA] hostesses and take them out. I used to say to them: 'Look, I want something in return – when you come back next time, please bring me a bottle of fresh milk.' And they would bring me two bottles of fresh milk.

All of which goes to prove what an innocent age and what an innocent place Gibraltar was in the late 1950s. And all of which you might think would have been unnecessary if they produced their own milk on the Rock. Was that a totally unreasonable thing to suggest? Surely a place with its own army, its own parliament and government, every bank you could imagine and Marks & Spencer could find somewhere for a dairy farm? It was a good question to ask – and, I should have thought, easy to answer. However, the answer was not so easy.

'Once upon a time', he said, as if telling a popular fairy story, which it turned out to sound like, 'we had a cow.' This was fascinating stuff. He was referring to Gibraltar's own cow, a real cow that chewed the cud and did most things a cow is expected to do; it was not an insult to a female for whom he had no affection. 'No, when I was a small child, there was a cow here. There was a soldier who used to cycle with this little can containing fresh milk for the governor. The cow died of solitude, so no more cows.' Perhaps somebody should have told that governor that cows needed – how does one put it? – refreshing every now and then.

But not everything is part of a fairy tale and not every item of edible or drinkable produce has to be imported. Momy and Sarah's daughter Kelly – her real name is Rachel, but for reasons which are difficult to define, this very Jewish young lady is known by everyone as the possessor of a very Irish name – is alone responsible for the popularity among Gibraltar Gentiles of smoked salmon bagels or cheese sandwiches on rye. (Actually, a reason did materialize in the course of our discussions: 'We used to call her Raquelita, the Spanish version of her name. But then we had an Irish nanny and she couldn't say Raquelita. So from day one the nanny called her Kelly.'

There are two other kosher restaurants which, amazingly, the Levy family allowed to get away and not be run by any of their incredible number of relatives. The Tamid is the only one that offers meat meals – which was why the Governor, Vice Admiral Sir Adrian Johns, chose it for a cosy tête-à-tête with Sarah, Momy and his own wife in the autumn of 2012.

And, according to the Levy family, people mix, Jews and Gentiles – but not as often with as many people as at one time. 'It has got a lot *frummer* here', Momy repeats time and again. 'But we go to parties and have tea together with non-Jewish friends.' Yet, plainly, because of the Jewish dietary laws, the parties are usually the ones that the Jews give, rarely the other way round.

Newcomers settle in a place which Momy maintains has several things to commend it – not least, the apparent lack of anti-Semitism. Or is it there? There have, for years, been social commentators who say such a thing is impossible. Even in Japan, a much larger country where there are fewer Jews than there are in Gibraltar, anti-Semitism has existed in some rather unpleasant forms. Well, Momy is prepared to accept that it is not as simple as that.

As he says, 'When my uncle was Chief Minister, relations between the Catholic and the Jewish community as a whole were always very, very close.' Momy's four daughters went to the local comprehensive school, but now there are private secondary schools – one for girls, one for boys, to which children go after completing their education at the Talmud Torah primary.

James was quite a sportsman – which he might not mind being told would surprise some people. His physique isn't exactly that of an athlete. But there was a time when he showed promise, and it was a promise fulfilled. He played football for Gibraltar in the under-13, -14 and -15 sides, and basketball, too.

He is married to Hilda, who came from Manchester and is 'very English'. And very religious: 'When I go to parties, by the way, people ask me: "How many children do you have?" So I say, "Six boys and five girls – all from one wife."' A well-educated wife who attended University College, London (James himself was at Manchester, having decided he didn't want to accept an offer to take up a place at Downing College, Cambridge).

It is difficult sometimes to separate his life from that of Momy. 'He's more independent in his life than I can be as a lawyer', says James. 'A lawyer is beholden to his clients and to issues, but Momy would have liked to have been one.' (We shall see why that didn't actually happen later on.) 'So when I bought my wig and gown the first thing he did was try them on himself. He wanted to see how he would look in them.'

Momy doesn't need to wear that wig and gown to make his point, says James;

> It's the way he deals with things. I can be in synagogue on Shabbat and it happens very often. He comes up to me and says to people, 'By the way, by the way, this gentleman ... this couple ... you have them at home for Shabbat, please?' I ring my wife. He invites everybody. He arranges things. He's got enthusiasm for social matters which matter. For instance, I was once worried about having the Ashkenazi Chief Rabbi of Israel in Gibraltar, because it meant serious and complicated security arrangements. But Momy rings up and says [we should have the party] in Marbella. He's got to come. So it means that I have to arrange it and I do. He's very enthusiastic for things which bring unity among people.

James continues,

> Friends love Momy because he always does the right thing – flowers for his wife on her birthday, cards. He remembers people. He's always increasing relationships among people. And he really does that very well. He's an expert on human relations. That's the way I'd put it. He works at it and becomes more efficient at it all the time.

It's a two-way street, Momy interrupts. He recalled a fairly recent serious illness that he had had: 'He was wonderful to me.' 'Oh no', protested James. 'I was only doing what he himself does to people. Not paying back, but just dealing with it, the way he does it.'

Now, after all that, it seems that the name Solomon Levy, on the plate outside his office or in correspondence with important people, means a paragon of all virtues. Not so, James admits:

> He calls a spade a shovel. When he doesn't like something, he will just say so – very clearly. I mean, for instance, if I've been out and I have not been given the message and I don't ring him he will call me and complain that he has rung twice and why haven't I rung back. I say I'm sorry. And then, immediately, there's no problem.

Momy is honest about his own position in life. His two brothers are, he says, 'more affluent than I am, bless them. But my way of life is higher than theirs.'

James agrees:

> He lives better than I do. He enjoys it. He lives better because he actually dictates the pace of his clients, not his clients dictate his pace. For instance, when he was president of the Jewish community here he decided what were his limits as president and how he would tackle that. And he just did what he had to do. He knows his limits and he will keep within those limits, even if it means he either doesn't please people or doesn't do something. And that's more honest than to try and please people when you can't. As president of our shul, he runs it with an iron rod. He doesn't take penny advice.

By which I took it that he meant that Momy knows the value of what people say – accepting what people say at the value he assesses. To which he himself says: 'If I don't think a thing is right, I go home.'

James says that he wouldn't go into professional politics because he hates speaking in public. But there was a time when he was very active in the local political scene. He actually founded a political party, which before long came to form the government. But without his actually winning a seat in Parliament. 'That was when my uncle's party was foundering.'

When he tells these stories, his elder brother positively glows with pride. Which is quite plainly a mutual feeling. Momy says, 'I'm very proud of him. He is very supportive. That means if anybody in the family needs help in any way, he is the first in line.'

There was a family tragedy and Momy (to use a popular cliché that may not have yet reached Gibraltar, since baseball is no more a national sport on the Rock than it is in Britain) stepped up to the plate. James explained: 'My son-in-law passed away, a terrible tragedy. And the first person I told was Momy.' 'When they took the body off the plane', Momy himself remembered, 'I sat in the car in front.'

The closeness of the brothers is noted throughout the community and outside, too. If they still had to go through a switchboard operator to talk to each other, he or she would know just how close they really are: Momy said, 'We speak to each other two or three times every day.'

'He's very loyal', says James. And that brother has an explanation for that: 'It is because of Papa and Mama. Otherwise I wouldn't be like that. Our father and mother, they taught us to be like that.' We shall see more of that later on.

It means that Momy always gets a seat at the top table at family functions (and more about that later on, too). 'He's head of the family', says James. 'He's good fun with the kids and [they] concentrate on him and ignore me.'

James recalls his earliest memories for me: 'When I was about seven and sort of perspiring from a football game, with a dirty football shirt, I met him in the street – looking very posh – with clients. He was very nice to me that day – but sort of kept me in my place.' There were other incidents, about which he has been told but which he doesn't actually recall. 'I don't remember', he emphasizes, and it would be remarkable if he did, but he said: 'When I was young, a year old or something, I used to sing "God Save The Queen". (Actually, it has to have been "God Save The King".) Momy used to bring his friends to listen – to me singing God Save The King.'

Of course, it is not possible to be completely sure of Momy's reasoning in organizing this one-baby concert. Was it simply to show the prodigious talent of his brother or an opportunity to hear what, as we shall see, is in effect the earlier version of Solomon Levy's theme song? I wouldn't like to guess.

The brothers are extraordinarily close. Perhaps it is because they certainly have so much in common – not least the belief that life doesn't have to be restricted to within the *eruv*, the notional boundary which, as we will see, allows religious Jews to carry on the Sabbath and mothers to use pushchairs.

The participation of the brothers in Gibraltar life is staggering. There is, for instance, Community Care – the largest charity on the Rock. James is the director.

> It was set up at the time of the Spanish pensions problem – when the Madrid Government decided not to increase pensions of their citizens living in Gibraltar because it would have involved liability for the Spanish Government.
>
> It's been attacked by Europe, by the British Government, by the Spanish Government, but we are carrying on – although we seem to be bombproof at the moment.

Momy, however, isn't sanguine about the Gibraltar of today. He returns again and again to the religious aspects of Jewish life:

> When we started to get the influx of certain people in black hats and dark suits and their influence, they [seemed to be] bringing to Gibraltar this orthodoxy which, as far as I am concerned, had

> never existed in Gibraltar before. I know we have to have progress. There's no doubt – but within limits So the community was trying not to split, but to separate a bit. When I became Mayor, I think I managed to bring people back together.

James is the first to agree with this:

> People have moved here and they are much more religious. I want to use the right word for them. Let's say they want to have a higher standard of Judaism. They are very committed, of course, but they're also very vocal sometimes about standards and things like that. So we have to manage that situation. They are good people. They're not aggressive people. So it's manageable. At the moment the community is very much on an even keel. Yes, we've moved to the right, fairly united, despite differences.

Life would be even better, Momy constantly says, if there were more mixing. Having to mix and actually doing so are two distinct things. Momy thinks people do mix. His close friend, Robert Seruya is not so sure. He is one of the shopkeepers who closes his establishment on Shabbat, although that really doesn't say enough. He is Gibraltar's perfume king and it seems as if every other shop in Main Street is his, although that is not quite true. Certainly, every waft of Chanel No.5, Arpège or any other brand that makes the street smell rather more pleasantly than most city centres in the world comes from one of the places where pretty girls, elegantly dressed and immaculately coiffured, can offer the gifts of the gods – but not the Jewish god. Seruya, with the voice of Oxford and the dress of Savile Row (although he won't claim to rival Momy himself in that regard) admits he has become very Orthodox. The Oxford accent is relevant – he was at school not a million miles from the city of gleaming spires with Momy, which is where their close friendship was first nurtured. But that is another story for another chapter.

Of course, none of this affects the commercial world of the Rock:

> Obviously in business you are open to the whole world. But it's socially I'm talking about. We keep very much to ourselves. It is the story of a small community. One of the virtues of [a community of this size] is that we are virtually like a little ghetto. It's very protective of its members – which has its good side and its bad.

One other side of that ghetto approach is another constant fear – not so much of getting too close to the non-Jewish world, but of being too different. There, Gibraltar *is* different. It's not like France where Jews are frightened of wearing their *kippot* (skullcaps) or even in London where one particular Jewish school has advised young boys to remove them when they go on the buses or trains home.

There's not just the influx of people from other parts of Europe to consider. According to Momy, the biggest group of immigrants comes from Spanish Morocco – 'where there's no religion'. But Seruya goes further: 'There are about 1,500 Moroccan workers here and they behave themselves.' Patronizing, perhaps, but the point is taken:

> The big secret [of the feeling of safety for Jews] is the matter of distance. If you are in trouble, everything is here. Everything is only 200 to 400 metres away from where you live. So it's like a large family. It's much easier than in Golders Green where you have to go a distance to take your kid to school or whatever.

Yes, I had heard it before. It was all in that same metaphorical siddur. And it had a great deal to do with the fact that, unlike small communities, say, in England, young people stay in Gibraltar without moving to more exciting climes, as Seruya explains:

> There are more opportunities for work here, to take your child to school, pick him or her up and go back home in that very short distance. Your control of kids is much easier here. The fact that

> you can let your child go down the street by himself or herself at the age of six or seven ... that's unheard of in England. But here, it's the norm – and they're particularly safe. We also lead an outdoor life. The weather permits that sort of outdoor life, which you in England don't have.

On the other hand, there is always the condition of familiarity breeding contempt. Surely, young people are not going to be content with just the boys and girls they have known all their lives? There was almost, at that point, a cue to the Morecambe and Wise line that there was no answer to that. Seruya took the point: 'Yes. that's the disadvantage. I was lucky – I married a girl who lived 100 yards down the street from where I lived. Both Momy and I would travel quite substantial distances to look for a wife – and yet we married two local girls.' On the other hand, there is another echo of the *Fiddler on the Roof* story here in Gibraltar – the role of the shadchan, the marriage broker. Or, as Seruya, by now warming considerably to his theme, put it: 'Generally speaking today, quite a number of marriages are arranged in this community.'

There is one disadvantage for this question of no distance being a problem. 'I can never have the excuse of a red light making me late. But it's a nice little place. Claustrophobic a little. But we can get away to Spain. We go to England reasonably often. It used to take us eight hours to fly from Gibraltar to London. We'd go via Madrid and then Bordeaux before we landed at Northolt Airport.' Today, that airport is essentially used for military and occasional VIP flights. 'In those days, the pilots used to drink. There were no accidents, but we'd have a pretty rough ride in those Dakotas.' Now Jews come to Gibraltar by easyJet and are there in a couple of hours. They come and seem pleased that they do. One of the examples of a happy community can be summed up by the word 'tolerance'. James Levy told me how his brother became a justice of the peace. 'I myself used to advise the

1. Momy's parents, Isaac and Rachel.

2. Momy, Nita and Abraham in Madeira.

3. The ever elegant Rabbi Kopul Rosen, Momy's mentor.

4. Momy at the wheel of his red MG in 1968 driving his uncle Sir Joshua Hassan (standing top right). The Chief Minister had just returned from the UN, declaring his determination that Gibraltar would remain British.

5. Momy meeting Israeli Prime Minister Menachem Begin. In the foreground is a future ambassador to Britain, Yehuda Avner.

6. 'Fire!' The last round on his last salute – 4 August 1978.

7. The first time a Governor attends a Barmitzvah in Gibraltar. General Sir David Williams greets Isaac.

8. On parade. Momy proudly carries the Gibraltar name plate at the annual Remembrance Day commemoration of the Association of Jewish Ex-Servicemen and Women.

9. Mr Mayor.

10. The Mayor presented with an inscribed shell case after the 21-gun salute.

11. The Mayor inspecting the gun-salute troops.

12. Brother James greeting the Mayor.

13. Momy's party for the Rock's taxi drivers.

14. Momy's second home – his office. Above his head are portraits of his parents and grandfather.

15. The orator. The Governor looks on.

16. Momy showing Vice Admiral Johns, the Governor, and his wife, round the 'family synagogue'.

17. Momy with his brothers, James and Abraham and the Chief Rabbi Lord Sacks.

18. What the rabbi said to the bishop. Momy brings together the four faiths – the rabbi, the minister, the imam and the bishop.

19. Guest of the Governor, Vice Admiral Sir Adrian Johns and Lady Johns (second right), at one of Gibraltar's kosher restaurants.

20. Farewell to the Countess of Wessex. Momy in his element.

21. Presenting the Earl and Countess of Wessex with a Diamond Jubilee painting.

22. Sarah and Momy with their children: from left to right, Rutie, Giselle, Kelly, Sarah, Momy, Isaac and Babsy.

23. The banner – Momy's gesture of loyalty.

24. Momy's favourite picture.

25. Mr Gibraltar.

From Lieutenant Colonel J C Perez MBE
The Royal Gibraltar Regiment
Devil's Tower Camp
British Forces Post Office 52

Tel: (+350) 2005 3057
Fax: (+350) 2005 3613
Email: perezj@a.dii.mod.uk

Mr S Levy MBE ED JP FRICS
3 Convent Place
PO Box 190
Gibraltar

Ref: RG/1330

4 August 2009

Dear Momy,

I had to write, on behalf of my men, to pass on my heartfelt thanks for your proud representation of the Regiment during your term of Office as Mayor of Gibraltar. It has been our honour to have one of our own serving in Office with such style, integrity and commitment to the people of Gibraltar. You have been a first class Mayor and have set the bench mark at its highest point. I am sure that your late uncle would have been very proud indeed. Your contribution has been immense. Let me also take the opportunity to thank Sarah for her sterling work and support in the background.

Two occasions will stand out for me as most memorable during your Office. Firstly of course, your return to the Gun Line on the Anniversary of Her Majesty's accession to the throne. Secondly, I will always keep with me the memory of your taking the Regiment's salute as we exercised our Freedom of the City. That the Mayor of the City can be counted such a friend of the Regiment encapsulates for me the essence of Gibraltar's spirit.

Although it is a pity that you must relinquish your office I am encouraged that you are succeeded by Olga Zammitt, whom I know also will be principled and proud.

I thank you once again, Momy, and I look forward to many more years of your companionship as a gunner, a soldier and a true friend.

Yours

26. Letter from Lieutenant Colonel Perez.

His Worship the Mayor,
Solomon Levy, M.B.E., E.D., J.P., FRICS.,
3, Convent Place,
Gibraltar

4th August 2009

Dear Momy,

I have just returned from my summer vacations to discover that you had passed on the "Baton" to your successor.

I would like to express my heartfelt gratitude to you for the exemplary manner with which you have fulfilled your task as its first Civic Mayor of Gibraltar. From the day of your inception you showed to have the enthusiasm and keenness to make a good job of the responsibilities presented to you.

May I point out that you have carried out your task with dignity, dedication and generosity. You have been open to people of all religions and of all classes from the outset. You pushed ahead the concept that in Gibraltar we respect one another whatever their religion. I am convinced that since you held that office as Mayor you have assisted in consolidating this reality. You should be very proud of this accomplishment.

Thank you again and may the Almighty bless you and your family, as he has been doing in the past, for giving of your precious time to serve us as Mayor of Gibraltar.

To end I would like to express my congratulation on your recovery. I heard you were in a Hospital in Benalmadena and that you are well and back at work.

God bless you.

+ Charles

Charles Caruana,
Bishop of Gibraltar

27. Letter from Charles Caruana, Bishop of Gibraltar.

government – not just this government, but the one before – and I used to spend more time on that than I did in my chambers. The Chief Minister at the time said we need to have more JPs and asked me how many the Jewish community had. I said: "They haven't got any. Call my brother in".' Thus began yet another job for Solomon Levy, Esquire. It was recognition of sorts – but more was to come.

Even now, the figure of Sir Joshua Hassan looms large over Gibraltar. Certainly, over the Jewish community in general and his family in particular.

James credits the founder of his chambers for his own success: 'I did my finals in a month because Sir Joshua needed me back. So I finished my degree in July, took a bit of August off and then started work. Now, they don't allow you to do that, because I didn't even know what to call the judge. I thought he was called "Your Majesty" or something.'

Every lawyer has a list of cases he enjoys talking about which wouldn't enter any of the tomes in his legal library:

> I was once doing a case involving a man called Gomez, who was always in the county court owing money. So I was cross-examining him for one of his finance companies. I mean, it was a joke. 'You haven't paid the £2 in a month', I said. He replied: 'Your Majesty, I haven't got the £2 to pay.' And he winked at me.

The Jewish community is not beyond what some would consider the more serious cases which come before the courts. Mr Justice Barrington Black, formerly a Leeds solicitor who became a London county court judge, is currently completing his second year sitting on the bench at Gibraltar's Supreme Court, to which he was appointed at the age of 80 (the oldest judge since that epitome of the British judicial world, Lord Denning), is not too happy at accepting social invitations from members of Rock Jewry – in case any of them turn out eventually to be 'customers'.

James Levy remembered a local Jewish boy he represented for possession of cannabis. The magistrate told him to stand up, 'because you have been convicted of a very grave offence'. 'The clerk pointed out that he hadn't been convicted yet, to which the worship replied, "Well, it's time he *was* convicted."'

Cannabis seems to have been a problem with Gibraltar's judiciary for a number of years. James and Sir Joshua appeared at the first of these cases – which attracted a full house of spectators. After telling a working photographer to 'Stand up, old man. I'm going to sentence you to two years in prison, suspended. He then said that every member of the 'audience' was going to be fined the maximum of £500. Their only 'crime' was to be sitting in the court at that moment. He later learned his mistake. It was no wonder that Momy was welcomed to the magistrates' bench.

Sir Joshua himself, says his youngest nephew, was a 'very human man'. Once, recalled James, he was consulted in a matrimonial case. The couple were constantly involved in arguments, but his uncle believed it was all due to the parents of one of the parties:

> 'Just a minute', said Joshua. And he goes to his drawer, takes out 60 quid or something like that, gives it to them and said, 'Look, go to Tangier for the weekend together and when you come back, you'll be a new couple. You go very well with each other.' They took the £60 and they never came back. That's the sort of thing he used to do. A wonderful man. He used to speak with the same humility to the dustman as to the Governor.

Most people believe that James's brother has inherited that gift of being 'very human'. If there were a serious problem, he would be there. If there were a problem and you needed him, he would be there.' His story fascinates his nephews. And well it should, since, as Momy says, he was the 'father of modern Gibraltar'.

Momy went on, telling what is as much a family story as part of Gibraltar's heritage:

> He had two sisters, one of whom was my mother. He went to England, qualified as a lawyer in the Middle Temple and came back to Gibraltar to practise on his own. He had, however, always had a flair for politics. In fact his office was knows as a social welfare centre rather than the domain of a barrister. All he had was a clerk, a manager and himself. Not like now, his office run by my brother James has eighty-three lawyers, 200 employees altogether.
>
> As soon as he came back from London, he took to politics here in a big way. The colonels and the brigadiers ran Gibraltar in those days. Sir Joshua said, 'Gibraltar should be for the Gibraltarians. We must run it ourselves.' And he started to campaign for Gibraltarian rules, as it is called.

It was through Joshua's efforts that the people exiled because of the war (see the next chapter) were able to come back and settle down:

> Nobody moved to bring them back. So he founds a party, the AACR, the Association for Advancement of Civil Rights. It is a group and he starts to make presentations to the British Government who say, 'All right, instead of having the majority of councillors who are army people, we'll have the majority of local people. And the chairman will be a Gibraltarian.' The chairman they chose was Joshua.

His first aim was to make it different from what had been rule by the Society of Commissioners. But that was after the first elections for a local authority. 'He must have been in his late 30s at the time', Momy recalls. 'They gave him the title of Mayor.'

He was a mayor with all the trappings – the blue-and-gold robes, the gold chain. Later on the Duke of Edinburgh came to Gibraltar to open the building which became the headquarters of the Legislative Council – which later turned into the Rock's House of Assembly and then the parliament in name as well as in function.

Sir Joshua was the proudest man on that side of the Mediterranean. Momy says:

> In the forty years he stood for elections, he always topped the poll. When they changed the constitution, he became Chief Minister and stayed in that office for eighteen years. So he was the most important person in Gibraltar for all that time. Only once in his time in politics was he defeated in an election. Just once two parties got together to get him out. So for eighteen months he was in opposition.

It had really all started in September 1942 when an association was formed by a trade unionist named Albert Risso. It wanted all those civilians who had been evacuated from the Rock to be allowed back – and able to continue their working lives, which had been interrupted by being sent away. They also wanted more civil rights. The Gibraltarian Association, as they called themselves, brought Joshua Hassan into their organization. He immediately suggested a more grandiose name, his Association for the Advancement of Civil Rights. It was in all aspects, if not in name, a political party, led by Risso. Hassan was vice president and took over from Risso in 1948 – which really marked the start of his rise to real prominence.

His term in office lasted from August 1964 to the same month in 1969. The two parties that had got him out formed a coalition. But that broke up, they held new elections and Sir Joshua was elected First Minister again.

The situation was such that, just as most people in Britain cannot imagine anyone but the Queen on the throne, it seemed impossible to imagine anyone but Sir Joshua Hassan being Chief Minister. When he finally retired, it appeared stranger than anyone could imagine. But people who had left the Rock at the time of his first election and who now came back would never have recognized it. What had formerly been a Crown Colony was now a British Administered Territory.

'It was my uncle who made all the changes work. We are still self-sufficient. The only thing we don't control [is] foreign affairs.'

How different it would have been with someone else in charge when Joshua Hassan first became mayor in 1955 (it should be emphasized that that wasn't really his debut; in 1950 he became a member of the Gibraltar City Council, and then chairman of the council, a role which was unofficially regarded as that of mayor) and Chief Minister in 1969 is a matter for conjecture. No longer was the rather small, rotund man with thinning (but once curly) hair there to deal with the sort of problems that a British prime minister would not consider in his remit at all. In addition to the statesmanship – and, with the continuing crisis with Spain, there was a great deal of that needed – local people would come to him with their difficulties. 'They would have so many things to complain about', Momy recalls:

> They would bombard him – 'Mr Hassan, I need a house. Mr Hassan, my drains are in a terrible state.'
>
> Those people and their descendants still remember the walks Sir Joshua took down Gibraltar's Main Street. A woman would come up to him and say, 'I'm sorry to tell you Mr Hassan, sorry Sir Joshua, but I've got this problem of this house. I've been complaining about it and nobody is paying attention.' He would make a note and then ring the head of the department and ask, 'What are you doing about these people?'

As Momy says: 'Joshua would talk to the scavenger the same way that he would talk to the Queen. No pretences about it.' There seems to have been a bit of hyperbole in that statement, but the general idea was there.

Indeed, all the evidence is that he dealt with the same regard as he showed for ordinary citizens (whom he recognized as his voters, it has to be said). He treated them no differently from the way he regarded the rich and powerful. Always, it seemed, his first priority was his fellow citizens (his loyalty to his co-religionists was always taken for granted, both by him and by the synagogue congregants):

> He had a very menial salary, but he didn't need money, his family had some property. Yet he battled with the British Government to get more and more powers for Gibraltar, which remained his object in life. And thanks to him, we have what is Gibraltar today. I'm not speaking as a nephew but as a Gibraltarian when I call him the Father of Gibraltar.

A father who, Momy maintains, literally travelled the extra mile, to achieve his aims: 'He went to speak to the Spaniards. But he never said yes to them. Truthfully, he never said no either. He just listened and spoke. He went to the United Nations several times to put Gibraltar's case.' That is an understatement. When he addressed the UN's Special Committee on Decolonisation, he made the most forceful speeches of his life, stressing how much his fellow citizens opposed Spain's claim.

Back home, he was the man who really changed Gibraltar's government for all time. The man who was nicknamed 'Salvador' ('Saviour') by his supporters was one of the principal drafters of the Rock's first constitution.

And his legacy lives on, as much as anything as a man who is still remembered as one who defends the rights of his people – and his family. Sometimes that is a difficult job to do. So often one gets subsumed by the other. But his family always had a place in his mind.

> He was a compromiser, a man, despite everything, the British Government loved. The only time he put his foot down was when

> Geoffrey Howe, the Foreign Secretary, ran after him to stop him leaving talks because they knew he was a very reasonable man.

Hassan was known by everyone, Jew or Gentile alike, and a man who, despite his position as the Rock's first citizen (the Governor represents the Queen), was very much part of the Jewish community. Even so, he never held an official position in the congregation, except that of being 'one of us', which would have given him any honour he would have liked to have heaped upon him. 'During the war, when most of the Jews had left Gibraltar, he was unofficially regarded as the president. But it was a strictly honorary position.' Indeed, they wouldn't have found anyone more honorary, or rather, honoured.

'He went to the synagogue every Shabbat, never missed one', Momy recalled. 'I used to love it when he was in the synagogue and the Governor or someone from what is now the parliament wanted to see him, they would send a message. He always replied: "Tell him to wait or come back in half an hour. I'm in service now." Possibly, he could have been reading the weekly portion of the Prophets for the congregation. He loved to do that. And because he loved to do it, it was always reserved for him when he did it in Spanish, once a year, on the eighth day of Passover.'

The synagogues are quite plainly Momy's pride and joy. They are friendly, informal places in which a line in the service could be read by a member of the congregation with the rest of the people responding as they usually would to a rabbi or *chazan* (cantor). Momy, being the well-dressed traditionalist that he is, would have liked a bit of the old formality, particularly when he went to one of the Spanish and Portuguese synagogues in London (his brother Abraham has just retired as their spiritual head) such as Bevis Marks, very much the Sephardi cathedral synagogue in the capital: 'They used to be the big boys. All high class. They'd all have the top hats on, morning coats. It's mostly disappeared now. Not a patch on it. Not a patch.'

Gibraltar is obviously an attractive place for Jews to choose to settle. Ask a question about this and Momy has a ready answer:

> It's not because we feel an obligation to contribute to the country. For Shabbat we have an *eruv*, which means we can carry things or mothers can push prams. When I was a bachelor if I wanted a drink sometimes, I could go into a bar, ask for a beer, say thank you very much, bye bye. I'd pay the next day. They know who we are. We know each other.

And, Momy stresses, it's part of the social fabric of Gibraltar:

> Yes everybody invites people on a Friday night [for the eve of Shabbat dinner]. It is a very pleasant tradition, especially when we are able to sit on a patio and enjoy dinner out of doors. We live in a flat, so don't have a patio, but my daughter has one and we go there or to friends' houses. And then, we ask people to our home. I like to be in my home on Shabbat, have my vino and then sleep. We have guests all the time.

And those guests bring with them their own traditions, their *minhagim*. That is a broadening experience in itself. In some families, it is traditional for husbands to sing to their wives (if they can stand it) a paean to a woman whose 'worth is far beyond rubies'. 'A few months ago', Momy remembered on my last visit to his home,

> we had a honeymoon couple invited to us on a Friday night. He sat down next to his new wife and sang to her. He didn't kiss her, just held out his hands to her. We thought it was out of this world. They were from London and it was so nice because he said, 'My voice is not too good ...'. But that didn't matter. He asked me to help him out. I knew what he was singing, but I wanted to hear him and it was wonderful.

The Sabbath is also an occasion to demonstrate Momy's idea of international relations:

> There are quite a few non-Jews here who are very pro-Jewish and they like to follow the Old Testament. Although they are not Jewish, I like to have them at my Friday night table, too. One couple said, 'Oh Momy. You can't imagine how delighted we are to come.' So I sang to them, gave them a book, pointed out the page and they followed our Shabbat service in English.

But Gibraltar Jewry really shows its best self at weddings. 'Thank God, we have a lot of them and everybody – and I do mean everybody – in the community is invited.' The *whole* community? 'Yes, the whole community. If you don't invite, then God beware!' Not that all 800 – or even 650 – will be able to accept the invitation. 'The population figure includes babies, old people, the sick, people who just wouldn't be able to go.'

James Levy sees the way his own community acts as one of its strongest points:

> The community is changing. First of all, it is one of the only communities in the world with old values. In the sense that you have here the old trades, the old Jewish opinions and observances under one roof. And we all cry together when we have problems and we all celebrate together – despite underlying ... I wouldn't call them tensions, but underlying differences.
>
> You have what you would call an ultra-Orthoodox man with a man who, if there were such a thing, would probably be affiliated to a Reform synagogue, going to the same weddings, the same funerals and the same functions and mixing and gelling together.

This, Momy recognizes, is one of the advantages of Gibraltar's size and geographical position: 'Now obviously, we can do that because of the size [of the place] but it's something that is very rarely seen in other communities. I think this was probably the case in Ireland when it had a more active community.'

And James, like the others I have spoken to, bemoans the fact that inter-religious relations are not what they used to be – even though he believes that the Jewish community itself is more united than it has ever been before. Maybe the fact that there is not the organized contact between the faiths in general – with the certain exception of the Levy brothers – is a symptom of a certain insecurity that never existed before. The influx of Orthodox co-religionists from abroad, and particularly from England, who were not used to even having non-Jewish neighbours in some cases, may have contributed to that. It is, in its extremes, almost a ghetto mentality. Despite that, the influence these two men exert in their own ways is very telling. For instance, every Gibraltarian knows that a Levy family wedding is a big occasion and some of them are in on the fact that the local rabbi was once seen to be dancing with his Church of Scotland opposite number.'

Momy's friend Robert Seruya is very conscious of the elder Levy brother's work and says, only partly tongue in cheek: 'As you have probably gathered yourself, he really enjoys his public relations work very much.'

James metaphorically takes off his *kippah* to his brother (although outside of his office he wouldn't dream of actually doing so). He says:

> It's a problem because this is a very small place here and relationships are very important – and therefore you really have to live not only in harmony and peace but in friendship and in deep friendship with others. Momy is seriously excellent at this. He makes more efforts than anybody else in the community to do that. Some of us manage to do that in our professional lives. We have here 80 lawyers and 180 staff. So it's a family of its own, but I always point out our Jewish ways. We have a kosher

> kitchen, for instance. That doesn't affect anyone else, but people know it *is* a kosher kitchen. We close for Shabbat. That doesn't affect anybody because a lot of people now work from home. I remember once a very gaudy client telling me, 'You can't be an international firm' – which we most definitely are – because we close on Shabbat and the *yomtovim* (the religious festivals). Nowadays, with the internet, it's a bit irrelevant, because of the ability to work away from the office.

It all helps, he maintains, to cement relations with the outside world: 'I must tell you there's respect for the Jews here. Very great respect for the Jews.' His uncle Sir Joshua Hassan experienced anti-Semitism only once, says Momy now: 'They had a demonstration when my uncle was in power several times – which, of course, is people's democratic right. The man who led the demonstration kept shouting, "Go back to Israel, Hassan". But that's very, very rare, thank God.'

Above all, the Gibraltar story is one of how people react to each other. Certainly, it is obvious that they try not to make what differences there are show when the 'family' of Gibraltar Jews get together, particularly at those weddings – not all of which are actually held in Gibraltar. Combine Momy's overseas family and friends, for instance, with the Jewish (and non Jewish) citizens of the Rock, and it might appear as though the place is in danger of toppling over into the sea. When James Levy had a wedding for one of his children, 600 to 700 people overran a hotel in Marbella.

The family are sufficiently well mannered to avoid the problems which people in other Jewish circles have experienced.

'You get people', said Momy, 'who complain. They get very offended. "Why should I be upstairs when I should be downstairs? Why should I be expected to sit at that table?" Thank God, that has never happened with me. As long as I can sit down and have a good meal, I don't care where I sit.'

I said that was because he was *always* given a good place. 'Well, as we say in Spanish, that's the gift of God.' Which is what he thinks people take away with them after attending one of the Gibraltar synagogue services. He admits he doesn't like being offered a seat in a shul – one of those where he is not president – that isn't in, let it be said, a prime position: 'If they do sit me in the second or third row, I must say, I do get a bit annoyed. I want to be sat in the proper place because of my age, because it shows respect for older people. But if I'm in the back, I do sometimes like that. If I want to leave early, I can just slip out.'

He likes seeing young children in synagogue. As much as anything, it gives him a chance to demonstrate his feelings about Children's Lib:

> In the old days when I was a child spoken to by an older person, I used to address them as 'Mr' or 'Mrs So and So'. I now love how young kids come up to me and say, 'Momy, Momy ... What's doing today?' The parents tell them off, for disrespect, but I tell them to shut up. 'You keep quiet, let the child speak.'

That, at least, is what he told me he says. Somehow, not having had the advantage of actually being present at such a confrontation, I doubt it. He is a seriously well-mannered fellow. He likes people to use the familiar Spanish word *usted* when talking to him, rather like the French *tu*. As he says, in 'the old days', he wouldn't have dreamed of doing that: 'But them doing it for me, I like. And I love being called Momy. It's a sign of still being young!' He was a mere 75 when he told me that.

As he added: 'We go to the shuls and we socialize there. And we are always meeting on other occasions.' Such as, in Momy's case, bumping into an elderly couple as they stroll down Main Street or a young mother, wheeling her new baby – always a good reason for a stop to chat. Not that Solomon Levy ever needs a reason or even an excuse to stop to talk, or even to walk and talk if he hasn't got time to actually stop.

Belonging to a synagogue helps in the big social scheme of things – and Momy believes it's worth paying for. 'I donate something like £500 a year for my wife and myself. It helps to run the synagogue.' But it is not the only income for these institutions. The community is well funded by donations. 'But every year, we are in the red – to the extent of £70,000 to £80,000.'

In British Orthodox synagogues, the annual fee covers the cost of burial. In Gibraltar, only the earth covers a grave – in a plot of land especially earmarked for Jewish burials. 'It is very expensive to die', says Momy. 'A lot of people bequeath money to the community in their wills. At the same time, you get a 24-hour service seven days a week.'

A burial could cost as much as £1,500, although the families of those who couldn't afford that could be charged as little as £50. But there are no undertakers to worry about. The great honour for families is to be able to personally lay the body in the grave, a tradition that might not commend itself in other parts of the Jewish world.'

That cemetery, like so much in local Jewish life, is very much part of Gibraltar's history:

> The first thing the Jews did when they arrived on the Rock was to buy land and build the Sha'ar Hashamayim Synagogue. And then they had the cemetery which is by what is now the airport and facing Spain. Then, they went to the Governor and said, 'Look, we are going to stay here. But we don't want to be buried opposite a place from which we were expelled in 1492.' So they were given a plot in the upper rock, which is still there, but not used any more.

That area, appropriately enough, is called Jews' Gate: 'It's where seven famous rabbis are buried. Every year, we go there to say Kaddish. The grass is cut and it is immaculate. Incidentally, by having a cemetery up there, the governor was happy. It made it seem that the Jews weren't supposed to be here, so it helped by them being out of sight.'

Even Momy agrees that that is not a nice situation: 'Once we were out of sight, Jews started buying property. At one stage, 60 per cent of property here was owned by Jews. So it's pretty awful that we are officially banned by the Treaty of Utrecht, 1713! When I talk to governors to complain, they jokingly say, "And you be careful now. Otherwise, I'll send you out of here."' Not with Momy in charge, they wouldn't.

The threat of leaving is, all too obviously, part of Jewish history if not of contemporary Jewish life. But establishing communities, in the pattern that Gibraltar adopted centuries ago, is very much part of Jewish religious tradition. And, according to James Levy, the Rock is more religious than ever. 'As we have said, it has become a lot more observant', he told me. 'Outwardly and inwardly observant.' But then, he points out, that is occurring in other religions too. Not just in local Judaism. For every Jew coming back to kashrut (the observance of the dietary laws) and the observance of the Sabbath, there is a Gentile, says the younger Levy. Returning to Christianity, he explains: 'It's a trend among Catholics here. There are a lot of new-born Christians here. I mean, I had a partner, one of my closest friends and not Jewish. He used to say, "If I see God, I'll punch him." And now, he's a very, very dedicated Christian. He goes to midnight mass.'

And that, for him, says James, is in his very lifeblood: 'People are, on the whole, religious because it gives them comfort, a feeling of well-being.' Yes, the Jews of Gibraltar have done well for themselves – and also for the Rock in general. Not only are they in government and in the professions and businesses, when it comes to supporting charities unconnected with Jewish or Israeli affairs (and there are certainly a lot of those), Jews are in the forefront, carrying out one of the principal precepts of the faith.

'Our good name is our proudest possession', says Momy Levy. And he certainly has reason to believe that – from both inside Gibraltar and outside.

He is proud of his relationship, not just with the MPs representing the people of the Rock, but also with a whole succession of Governors whom he treats with friendly respect and who themselves offer a similar relationship to Momy and the community he loves to represent.

When the Earl and Countess of Wessex came to Gibraltar as part of the Jubilee tour in 2012, Momy presented them with a painting of the Queen produced by a local artist, Christian Hook, the same man who had painted Momy's own portrait in his mayoral robes. It was, he says, Gibraltar's Jubilee gift. The next day, he will relate with the speed with which he signs a cheque to one of his estate agency clients, he saw the royal couple outside the Governor's palace, known incredibly as The Convent. The Countess spotted Momy and went up to him to say goodbye. 'A lovely lady', he said. She obviously had done the right thing to justify the epithet.

You will see the photograph in Momy's office, which is a cross (forgive the word) between an archive and what appears to be a compost heap. He will tell you he knows exactly where everything is and, time after time, put to the test, he is right.

Not only does he have his estate-agency files, but there are models and pictures – of his heroes and heroines, the Queen first (he has a working model in his office front window of Her Majesty waving to her adoring Gibraltarian subjects); then there are cases of model soldiers (including a squad of French troops which he bought when he went to Paris as part of the delegation from Britain's Association of Jewish Ex-Servicemen and Women), awards from the Royal Gibraltar Regiment to their honoured son, and displays of Laurel and Hardy, whom he loved. He bought those models – one of them with the faces of George Bush and Tony Blair underneath their bowler hats – on a trip to

Hollywood. Other figures of the pair he bought ... in Israel. 'I have lots of DVDs of them.' It was something for which he would have given his eye teeth years ago:

> When I was a child ... Laurel and Hardy and Abbott and Costello (I used to laugh like mad at Lou Costello, the fat one) were my four favourites – until I got to appreciate Tyrone Power and Anne Blythe; I loved Tyrone Power although I am by no means gay and I love his daughter Romina Power who was very famous on Spanish television.

More of that later. There are also certificates and letters of appreciation from bishops and rabbis and government ministers in London, who are glad that whenever the question is asked, he will find the proverbial (and maybe a real) soapbox on to which he will stand and proclaim his loyalty to Great Britain.

There are few surprises about Momy. You know that he is going to get those certificates and will display them. It just stands to reason. It is not difficult to imagine any of those models or anything in praise of the Queen making him as delighted as a schoolboy being picked for the first eleven. Certainly, after his family and his religion, the relationship with his native land borders on being a love affair. Of course, it's the place he loves most. Nevertheless, get him in a pensive mood and he will allow his thoughts to stray to the seemingly impossible. He knows London, where he trained for his business career, almost as well as he knows his home town. But he says that if the unthinkable happened and Jews were persecuted on the Rock, there is only one place to which he would want to go – Israel: 'If I couldn't live here and I had some money, so I could afford to take it easy and live on my money, that's where I would want to go. Now, at my age, I want to live comfortably.' But as we shall see, he says, in Gibraltar:

> I live like a king. I have enough to eat and I spend as I like because at my age, I don't know how much longer I'm going to last and I want to enjoy life. But if I had a lot of money, then I would consider having six months here and six months in Israel. But for me, Gibraltar really is home. I always say, I was born in Gibraltar and I will die in Gibraltar.

There would be no doubts about which side he would support in a sporting match. The famous 'cricket test' of the veteran Tory politician Norman Tebbit 'just wouldn't apply. I'm a British Gibraltarian. And if it were Gibraltar versus Israel I'd ... [he thinks for a minute] have to say Gibraltar.' No question of dual loyalties when it comes to someone called Momy. And then he finds a way of synthesizing the link between what to some people is still considered to be the 'motherland' and his religion. As he says: 'Every minute of every day, when I get up, I say as I pray the *Shacharit* service, "Thank God for Britain – and thank God for the British blood I have flowing in my veins."' A haematologist might not be able to identify that particular factor in his blood, but it is easy to see what he means.

That is shown in another display in his office – the literally hundreds of pictures that line his walls, with coloured portraits of his wife, parents and grandfather in pride of place. And if you want the story of Momy's life – or rather did want it before this book was published – the photographs tell it all. There is an enormous portrait of Momy in his mayor's robes, surrounded by Sarah, his children and grandchildren. You can see him driving his uncle the First Minister Sir Joshua Hassan in his favourite sports car (more of this, too, later). There are pictures with Israeli Prime Minister Menachem Begin and with Margaret Thatcher – and, inevitably, bowing to the Queen as she presented him with his MBE. Pictures, too, of him marching in his overcoat and bowler hat (the black one; he has bowlers in blue and brown which he alternates for wearing to synagogue on the Sabbath and Holydays) on those Sundays when he 'stars' at the Jewish Remembrance Day parade at the Cenotaph in Whitehall. Inevitably, in Gibraltar itself you will also see pictures of him with members of the local Royal British Legion, leading the branch as its proud chairman.

Pictures with the Governors – one in the navy, as now; one in the army; others in the Marines and the RAF – are there too, of course, and he'll tell you the story of each at the drop of a ledger or a parliamentary minute book. That is, until he is interrupted by a call on his mobile phone, with the ringtone of Israel's National Anthem, 'Hatikvah'.

Oh yes, there is one other passion – Arsenal football club, whose posters also decorate his office and whose flag flies outside it. The club once printed in their programme a whole-page paean to the 'Gunners' that he had written. Why Arsenal? Of course, he won't come out with it himself, but is it beyond the possibility that it has something to do with their colours – red and white?

Man on the Rock? This is The Man. Mr Gibraltar.

THE BOY

He has always been one of the pillars of our community in keeping good relations with the other parts of Gibraltar, the other religions.
James Levy

Ask three people about happiness in childhood and you'll get three different answers. Jewish people might give you six different answers. As Tevya said in *Fiddler on the Roof*, 'On the one hand ...'. And, of course, those hands sometimes don't need many words to go with them. Momy, looking back, needs the help of those hands quite considerably. But, unlike the *Fiddler* characters, he can come to certain conclusions – and all of them, from his point of view, were pretty good.

For Momy Levy, his sister Nita and brother Abraham, childhood wasn't exactly idyllic, but – on the other hand – they were a trio of happy youngsters living a kind of adventure. If there were clouds on the horizon – and, indeed, the clouds were pretty black as war first threatened and then came about – they were shielded from them. There was also an all-prevailing factor: the love of their parents, Isaac and Rachel. Momy adored them. In fact, he several times told me of a deal he tried to negotiate with the Almighty: 'I used to say, "God. Take five years from my life and give it to them."' As he told me:

> We were very fortunate in that we had parents who were utterly selfless and with tremendous integrity and my father was the man

> who provided authority in the house and my mother was the one who provided elegance and spiritual warmth. We have tried to follow their example. We are blessed in that we have a very united family, always working together and helping each other.

Such deals rarely work out and the inevitable happened. But that was many years later than their childhoods and the guiding influences of their parents persisted even after their deaths. You only have to see the large coloured portraits on the wall of Momy's office to realize that. As he said:

> You know, we like to think that every mother and father were good. But ours were very, very special. I learnt a lot from them. And I try to instil what I learnt to my grandchildren. I want all of them to thank God. I feel I have a mission in life to show that we Jews are all the same and we have to bring peace among ourselves.

His father was a very religious man. His influence in that was undoubtedly passed on to his children. To most people, Momy is a very religious man. But, as he pointed out, James is much *frummer* than he is himself and that goes for his sisters, too – to say nothing of his and their children. About that, Momy says: 'I'm quite happy the way I am, but my father always said, "the son must be one up on the father".'

But not necessarily one up on the mother. Momy admits that he aims to have his mother's standards. They were due to the influence of the husband upon his wife, he recalls.

> When she used to address my father, she used the respectful word for 'you', 'usted', because he was older. She was a religious lady who taught me the way I had to behave. And I know to this very day that it is because of her that every Friday before Shabbat I give charity – with two boxes in my office and eighteen at home

> for money for the good causes. And I do that in her honour. Every day, particularly on Shabbat, she dressed beautifully; she used the money she had been left in a family legacy – and that, I think, is why I dress well.
>
> She was a real lady in the true sense of the word. She was like royalty to us, yet very down to earth. She brought us up the way that she should and not once did she or my father smack us. And because [of] what they did during the war, the Almighty has been kind to my brothers and sisters and myself, responsible for the way we live now. It's a recompensation, as we say in Spanish. We have always been a very ordinary family, very modest when I was young, but thank God, I do have that very happy life.

And a happy Orthodox Jewish life, despite what he says about the degrees of Orthodoxy practised by his brothers and sisters. But, yes, it isn't quite as strict as that observed by the newer influx of young people, which is quite unusual in a Sephardi community.

James, the father of eleven children, echoes his father's influence: 'My father was a very interesting man. The three of us have had public profiles in a different way. My father never had any public profile.' To which Momy added: 'He was a hugely intelligent man – better than all of us put together.' That has to be seen as a combination of loyalty and filial devotion. They are proud to know that, like themselves, he was something of an internationalist. He went to school in Frankfurt am Main and was a fluent German speaker:

> He went to France first. My father was a very clever boy. And my grandfather didn't have a penny to his name. But he was very well known and respected by people who realized that he was Jewish.
>
> He had a brother, Isaac Levy (one of the several Isaac Levys) who said, 'I'm going to send your son to school in Germany.'

So Isaac, born in 1898, went to the Real School in Frankfurt. He was, by all accounts, doing very well there, but the First World War interrupted his studies and he had to return home. He started work in a solicitors' office, but qualified as a notary public, rather than as a lawyer himself.

The love of son for father is echoed by Momy's own 43-year-old son, another Isaac, who knows just how much Momy's father meant to him: 'He showed an incredible respect for his own father. Anything that his father did, he never questioned.'

Public personality or not, there's no doubt, however, that the senior Levy was a remarkable man who would have been an equally remarkable force in his community, had he wanted to be. However, his philosophy dictated that he didn't have to tell the world about the things he did. 'He gave charity privately', said James, 'to an amazing extent – but with little publicity, and he was pilloried for that. And I suffered as a boy, knowing that.'

Which prompted the question of why he was pilloried and why his son suffered. James had the answer as readily as if he had just dealt with a problem and found the solution in one of the magnificently bound law books lining his study. 'People thought he was mean with his charitable donations. They asked: "Why does he not make an offer of more than £5 [at synagogue or other charity appeals]?"'

Their mother, Rachel, sister of Sir Joshua, had an even less public persona than her husband. Her grandmother had come from France. Her paternal family, the Hassans, hailed originally from Manchester before settling for a time in Morocco – which was, as we have seen, the usual Jewish route.

Whether they spoke about roots – not routes – in his early childhood, Momy can't now recall. But it was not just the relationship with Sir Joshua for which this branch of his mother's clan had claims to fame. Her grandfather's mother was a member of the de Cansino family. Well, perhaps that needs to be said again, she was a Cansino. Possibly that will have resonance only with people of a certain generation – and people who loved the cinema of the war years, at that. A certain Margarita Cansino, a red-haired beauty, daughter of the iconic Spanish dancer Eduardo Cansino, was one of the great stars of the era, whom Momy might well have seen on the screen when he and his siblings were allowed to go to the movies. This was his somewhat distant cousin, better known as Rita Hayworth. There is a Cansino crest, which Momy will show visitors as willingly as any of the other proofs of his life's adventures. Whether Ms Hayworth ever knew about it isn't on record – nor did she, for some strange reason, boast about her relations, the Gibraltar Levys. Plainly, she had other things on her mind – lesser problems, like showing Fred Astaire that she could dance better than Ginger Rogers (which she undoubtedly could), getting more money for a film or fending off the advances of her boss, Harry Cohn, the head of Columbia Pictures (who invented the famous 'casting couch' and who on one occasion bugged the dressing room of one of his principal male stars, Glenn Ford, because he believed the actor and Rita were engaging in activities not covered by their Columbia contracts). No, it is surprising how the major things in life like getting to know Momy or even his brothers become subsumed in the minutia of Hollywood life.

Momy's mother did not speak a great deal about the star of films such as *Gilda* (that was the big one for her) and *Pal Joey*. Probably, the fact that the star – wife of, in turn, Orson Welles and Prince Aly Khan; the gorgeous woman who co-starred with Gene Kelly and Frank Sinatra – never claimed to be Jewish might have had something to do with it. This was not the kind of example of Jewish womanhood of whom the matriarch of the family would have liked to boast.

She and her own siblings were left some money from their mother, but that was not something she would talk about either.

Nobody has suggested that her reluctance to be more involved in communal affairs was because of her education, but perhaps when a very religious Jewish woman spends her entire school life being taught by nuns, that could have something to do with it. But that was not an unknown situation where they lived. 'My two sisters had all their education with the nuns, too', said Momy. 'Their schooling was really first class. Those sisters [and he is not talking about the nuns] both married rabbis and when they go out and talk about their education, they say they learnt French, English and Latin – all from nuns and "we are rabbis' wives". That was what Gibraltar was all about.'

Being educated by nuns provided certain problems for Jewish girls, but there were ways around them:

> In no ways did the nuns or the Christian Brothers, with whom both James and I spent time in the classroom, try to indoctrinate us. They used to say, 'Every hour we say Hail Mary. If you want to leave the classroom you can; otherwise you stay here.' [This was always the practice in British state schools.]
>
> I remember my mother telling me a story about when there was an anti-Semitic girl at the school. She was thrown out of the school because of that.

It was a good enough reason for Rachel Levy to think affectionately of the nuns. 'One of them lived to be 95 and religiously [to coin a phrase] my mother would go to see her. I used to drive her to have tea with her nun. They were really excellent. When the nuns and the Christian Brothers left, it was a great loss to their former pupils – and a great loss to all of Gibraltar.'

Both of their schools packed up at the same time. 'There were some left behind in a private school, still called The Convent. But there were very few of them, very, very few. When we started comprehensive schools on the Rock, they just left Gibraltar. It was such a shame because they were really A-1 teachers.'

James was also educated by the Christian Brothers, who ran what were reputedly the best schools on the Rock, while Momy and Abraham were at Carmel College in England – about which more later. Ironical, considering the Levy connection to the local Jewish community. But James, in particular, sees no reason for irony: 'Sir Joshua was educated by the Christian Brothers.' James had more than a conventional education from the brothers. On one occasion, he was fairly severely beaten by them – the term was 'six of the best', which for a schoolboy is pretty severe. He couldn't understand why he deserved such treatment. He says: 'I was told it was not for what I had done, but for what I was going to do.' It's an old story, but he swears it was true. Nevertheless, he says he bears no grudges. Today, his firm acts for the brethren.

James was born in October 1950, which means that he was not part of what his brothers consider to be the defining period of their childhood. They also regard the month of October to be particularly significant. Momy himself was born on 26 October 1936, a year before Nita. His wife Sarah's birthdate was 16 October 1946; their son was born on 29 October in 1969. His father's birthdate was 25 October and James was born on 23 October.

Abraham, who – as we have seen, and unlike his brothers – didn't stay beyond childhood in Gibraltar, starting to break the trend when he was born in 1938. Sadly, for the sake of what would have been a very good story, his birthday is not in October. He plainly has no memories of pre-war Gibraltar. As for Momy, any memories he does have of life on the Rock when there was talk of the coming conflict are extremely sketchy. But then, he was barely 2 years old when the infamous Munich agreement was signed, after which everyone was still talking about the Nazis and the possibility of hostilities. As the following year moved on, the possibility turned into probability. Even if the two boys and their sister had been old enough to understand, which patently they were not, the senior Levys shielded them from what could have been any worries. It was something they did all the time. Childhood, they both agreed, was not for grown-up problems.

Gibraltar was in what seemed at the time a precarious position. There it was, politics aside, an adjunct to Spain, a country whose sympathies were plainly with Germany and which could, circumstances permitting, join in what was about to be called the Axis (Germany, Italy and Japan), the moment it looked good for General Francisco Franco to act – and, with the kind of German help he had received in the Civil War which had just finished, march into the tiny speck of rock that Britain held so precious. The apes had to be protected; as we have seen, Churchill was adamant about that. But, more important, so had the fortress which dominated the Straits that bore its name. It was an intensely guarded outpost of the empire, the scene of battles of the past and it was hard to imagine that there would not be battles there in the future.

The British were prepared – more so than they had been in other what became known as 'theatres of war', although there was little theatrical about soldiers in rough khaki uniforms – the sort of dress to which, generations later, Solomon Levy would refuse to give houseroom, let alone wardrobe space. It wasn't like that other city state, Singapore (at the time part of Malaya), manned and armed to the hilt, but overcome by supposedly weaker Japanese forces, who simply entered the colony from the rear while the British guns were facing the sea in the opposite direction.

Momy and his brother and sister were too young to think about such things. They had left Gibraltar behind by the time the troopships docked at the Rock's harbour. They didn't watch – and even if they had, they wouldn't have known what they were seeing – guns and armed trucks trundling their way to what had been the colony's own racecourse. It was converted, more speedily than anyone could have imagined possible, into an airport. Every week, hundreds of planes took off and arrived at this make-do air base. A few years later, Momy would have loved to have seen the bombers and transport planes flying in and out, ready to go into action. As things turned out, it was to be more of a centre for a deterrent than a setting-off point for actual battle.

By war's end, Gibraltar hadn't suffered nearly as much as was expected. There was just one bombing raid that caused loss of life, although the enemy did make attempts at getting close enough to drop explosives, but it was difficult for them – plainly, the Germans were frightened of a bomb going astray and hitting Spain instead of the Rock. After all, bomb aiming was hardly surgical in those days (and still isn't always). There could have been another reason for the lack of serious bombing. The Nazis wanted the place intact, for the same reason that they wanted the Channel Islands to be preserved. There was a huge psychological dimension to the idea of Nazi troops marching in a country with British policemen in British-style uniforms and red letter boxes and telephone booths. Hitler asked General Franco for permission to march through Spain to Gibraltar and the Spanish dictator refused.

But it was not just the Rock itself and its military installations that had to be protected. So did its civilian population. The 2,000 Jews then living on Gibraltar were already getting worried. Nobody yet contemplated a Holocaust, but news of German Jews being carted off to concentration camps such as Dachau and made to do humiliating things such as cleaning pavements with toothbrushes had not just leaked out, but was already part of the currency of foreign affairs. Indeed, at that stage, the Nazis quite clearly revelled in the publicity they were getting for their nefarious deeds.

The need to leave seemed paramount for a swathe of the Jewish population. Before long, however, with the final decision of Neville Chamberlain to put his umbrella in the Downing Street hall rack and declare war on Germany, the question was taken out of their hands (both of them). The Churchill government ruled that the entire civilian population should be evacuated. They were worried about their being too close to any possible enemy action. Not only was there the risk of civilians being wounded or killed, but also (although this would never be admitted) of them quite simply getting in the way.

The British Government insisted that every civilian had to go to Casablanca, just across the water in French Morocco. The only exception was for men who were eligible for service in the army, the fire brigade or the civil service, or for those whose work otherwise helped the war effort.

It wasn't the city of the Warner Bros film, although – just as in the movie – it was a haven for refugees from all over what would soon become Occupied Europe. But Isaac and Rachel Levy never ventured close to the kind of establishment that Humphrey Bogart ran at Rick's, and the real Casablanca was so different from the whitewashed place in the movie. There may have been murders in the film but the bloodshed was in sharp contrast to the snow-white buildings which matched the equally white and immaculate suits, tuxedos and dresses worn by the stars in the film, to say nothing of the uniform of Claude Rains, the actor who played the local police chief. Besides, no one seemed to be playing 'As Time Goes By' and, look where you will, there was no Paul Henreid to sing *La Marseillaise*. Worse still, not even a lookalike for Ingrid Bergman.

The buildings were, in most parts of the city, as dirty as the clothes worn by the residents – crumbling apartments, and shacks occupied by the beggars who littered the streets, hunched as they offered open hands to the richer citizens of the city who had been negotiating deals in the carpet warehouses. There were, of course, those better-off citizens living in the better-off areas of Casablanca, and it was to one of those areas that the Levy family went and started to set up home. Momy has no real memory of any of that. 'We were refugees, really.'

One can only presume that when they took a house in their new home town, the children regarded it as some kind of adventure. Indeed, before long, they settled down to a comfortable enough short stay in Casablanca, which offered a friendly face to the family – particularly since, at that stage, they were not exactly poor. But there wouldn't be any call for Isaac to further his career as a notary public – which the *Encyclopaedia Britannica* defines as 'a public official whose chief function in common law is to authenticate contracts, deeds and other documents by an appropriate seal. [In some countries] the civil law notary can roughly be described as a lawyer who specializes in the law relating to real estate, sales mortgages, and the settlement of estates, who is not allowed to appear in court.' It sounds complicated, which it probably was, although there were a few other things to keep him occupied while in 'exile', although, as we shall see, not nearly enough. Money was draining through his pockets like water from a leaky bucket, although there were the rents from a couple of buildings in Gibraltar to provide a certain amount in savings.

Momy says about his father's business venture: 'Because we had some properties in the family he became a so-called part-time estate agent as a sideline'. (His father had built up his business himself – his own family had once been very rich, including a great-uncle, also named Isaac Levy, but he had gone bankrupt.)

For Isaac Levy, it was not an easy, steady climb to financial success. 'On one occasion', Momy recalled, 'he and his cousin, Solomon Levy [one gets to see how the family names become interwoven with each other], were going to try to solve the problems of the family business when they had a car crash travelling between Lisbon and Seville. The cousin was killed. My father's properties helped his financial situation during the five years of war when he was not able to work: Yes, the rents were still coming in from Gibraltar. He had left my uncle to run it.'

His sons don't have any real memories of Casablanca, except of the kind of event that no child would ever forget:

> One day I went to an aunt. I went in the lift – and it broke down. I was stuck for three-and-a-half hours. Ever since then, to this very day, I hate being in lifts. Unless I have a mobile phone with me and there's a good light there, I won't go in a lift. When I started to work as an estate agent, I would walk up ten floors – because there was no porter there, no one who could have rescued me if I got stuck in the lift in the building.

Not an elevating experience, you might say.

But a significant change took place in their lives: they were told they would have to leave. France had surrendered and this part of the French Empire, as the movie *Casablanca* clearly demonstrated, was now part of Vichy France, the collaborative regime presided over by Marshal Philippe Pétain. The British Government ordered them to quit what was considered to be enemy, if not occupied, territory. For Jews, the prospect of a Nazi-supporting regime, even though there would be little persecution during the war of the Moroccan Jewish community, was too bad to contemplate. The wandering Jews (and other Gibraltarians) were having to wander again. But where should they go? For a time they were back in Gibraltar. But they knew they would have to leave the Rock once more.

'They gave us the choice of London, Northern Ireland, Jamaica or Madeira', said Momy. My father decided we should not go to bomb-torn London, and the other places didn't have much to tempt them. The Levy parents considered their options and made their decision: they would go to Madeira.

A letter to Isaac Levy came from the British consulate in the Madeiran capital, Funchal. It was dated 13 August 1942. In this, the Vice Consul wrote that 'there is no objection to you, your wife and three children being included in the "B" category scheme for members of the Jewish faith from August 15, next'.

So they were all set. The difference was that, had they chosen one of the other places, they could have gone at the government's expense. To go to the luxury isle of Madeira, they would have to pay for themselves. Momy was sorry to see that the families of a lot of his friends had plumped for London, which was not exactly a peaceful alternative to what they imagined life in Gibraltar would be: 'Some would be in Jamaica and they had a rough time of it.'

The choice of Madeira seemed obvious for Isaac Levy and for the best part of 1,000 other people – including 200 Jews – who chose to go to the island. For those 200, it was a chance to establish a place in Jewish history. They were the first Jews to settle in bulk on Portuguese territory since the Inquisition and the expulsion which followed.

Isaac Levy took advice before he brought his family to the island. His grandson and namesake, Momy's son Isaac, produced for me a telegram sent to a cousin living in Lisbon – Abraham Levy at Rua Castillo in the city: 'HAVE YOU ASKED AMZALAK [Abraham's brother-in-law, Moses Bensabat Amzalak, who was said to be close to Portuguese government figures, including supposedly, the president] ANY FRIENDS WHO COULD ADVISE AND PROCURE US MODERATE LODGINGS?' The point that he was after 'moderate lodgings' gives some indication of his concern for the family's future financial situation.

'We had some expenses from the government', Momy remembered. In a way, Lisbon, and Portugal in general, was something of a transit centre, although a great number of the Jews who managed – and it wasn't easy, to say the least – to get out of German-occupied Europe chose to spend the entire war in the country. But, said Momy,

> the reason was that Portugal was neutral and had maintained they would stay neutral, my father believed it would be peaceful there. But my father couldn't work there, which meant that eventually there would be considerable financial sacrifices. Thank God, he managed to keep his family together and contented. How he managed to keep his mind going, I have no idea. It's a miracle.

But he did keep in touch with the solicitors' firm to which he was attached and which managed to stay afloat, despite the British restrictions on civilian activities. One imagines that closing down the law firm would have been a step too far:

> He used to write to his boss on legal matters – by hand; he didn't own a typewriter. The solicitors would continue to ask questions and he would answer, keeping a copy of everything he wrote. No carbon paper there. Everything was written out twice. Remember, they used to write back to him, saying, 'Levy, although you're miles away, you haven't forgotten all about English law.'

They first of all stayed at the Savoy Hotel, which was close enough to luxury on an island that was totally unaffected by war. The furnishings were attractive and so was the view from the hill above the sea. There was all the (permitted) food they could eat, although no kosher meat or poultry, of course. They stayed there for almost a year. 'But we couldn't live in an hotel interminably, so we started to look around and started to rent houses, before we found one to stay in for as long as we were on Madeira.'

The island was considered to be part of metropolitan Portugal. It was a delightful place. The Iberian atmosphere meant that it was not too unlike Gibraltar. The language was different, but anyone fluent in Spanish could work on it: 'Some people spoke English, of course. We got on very well. In fact, when we left, people said to us, "Since you've been here, you've brought us luck".'

But it wasn't Jewish – and, even more significantly, it wasn't British, although Winston Churchill had loved to go there. He stayed at Reid's Hotel, which was indeed Britain transplanted into this section of the Atlantic Ocean. Even then, with war declared and Britain standing alone (which, it must now be admitted, was a useful propaganda phrase, considering that the countries of the empire were sending their troops in full force and there were soldiers and airmen from Poland, France and other overrun countries), people still took tea and finger sandwiches at Reid's, and the cakes were still being served from silver-plated stands. The park overlooking the sea was one of the most attractive in that part of the world, leading to the hotel and its main competitor, the Levys' temporary home, the Savoy. The pavements were still beautifully patterned, the shops attractive. So this was where Momy's family and the other Jewish refugees made their home and were as happy as anyone could be away from their own normal surroundings. As far as the children were concerned, this *was* home.

A special school was created just for the Gibraltar children, one where the lessons would be given in English. 'We had teachers from Gibraltar who taught us a great deal about British history.' But not about Judaism. Like the schools on the Rock, it was very much a Catholic institution: 'Nothing exciting about it. It was good to get back home at the end of the day.' On reflection, however, Momy amends that. There *were* things to remember: 'They managed to get a building which was vacant and some of the teachers were English who came over along with the Gibraltarians. I still remember the name of one of my teachers – a Miss Costa.' He thought again. He remembered another name, Mr Formosa. One other thought struck Momy: 'It was at that school that I learned my English.' Until that moment, everyone in the Levy household spoke in Spanish, and only in Spanish.

He also remembered details of the staff at home – yes, they still had those, too: 'We had a maid and a fellow who was a handyman for us.

I'll never forget that after he left us he became the usher at the entrance of the Solar cinema, taking the tickets. When he saw me, he said, "Now Momy", which I knew meant he was going to let me in for nothing' – possibly to see his distant cousin Rita Hayworth, although he says that the small movie theatre specialized in old Portuguese films. But there were Hollywood pictures, too, occasionally: 'I remember towards the end I saw one with my favourite film star, Tyrone Power – *Blood and Sand*.' It was a picture about bullfighting – and I, too, have reason to remember it, but this is not the place to go into that. Says Momy: 'I now think of it as the first business deal I ever conducted – getting something for nothing, literally.'

The fact that the film had an English-language soundtrack made it preferable to the Portuguese movies, which gave Momy reason to be grateful for the success of the first talkie, Al Jolson's *The Jazz Singer*, which probably played at the Solar less than twenty years before Momy got his free seats there.

'Well, it was Tyrone Power for me – and his daughter Romina. She was the spitting image of her father.' He began to 'collect' his favourite stars – he rattles off the names: John Payne, Betty Grable and Alice Faye. And Boris Karloff, too. 'I love seeing the old films on television, and also, when I see one on DVD, I buy it.' Another Momy toy, but with an artistic touch. If psychiatrists say that one's life in childhood influences one's adult behaviour, surely Momy's trips to what used to be called the 'pictures' is perfect confirmation of the fact. Obviously, the cinema made a very big impression on Momy. He even remembers the name of the owner of the Solar: 'He was a very affluent man.' But the usher at the door wasn't. He was a youth named Manuel, like the less obliging one in *Fawlty Towers*. During the day, this Manuel still used to help in the house and chop wood. In the evening, he tore up tickets. What the proprietor thought of the arrangement by which there were no tickets from Momy to tear can only be imagined.

The trips to the cinema fitted in well with the family's stay in Madeira, which seems to have been a good, peaceful time. 'In five years, we never saw a plane fly by', Momy recalls. That meant that the siblings' other great source of enjoyment was never interrupted: 'We used to go to the park very often.' It was, indeed, a beautiful park, made more so by the equally beautiful weather. From the rolling hills inside what could seem to be a huge garden, they could look down on the ships in the harbour below. Today, they are mostly cruise ships, but in those days they were usually a few grey-painted vessels of the Portuguese Navy, defending the country's outposts from possible attack by countries on which they could rely, for the moment, to respect their neutrality, but they were never really certain who was a friend and who was about to stab them, metaphorically, in the back. Of course, Isaac Levy had no idea of the politics of it all. He could not possibly have realized the real value of Portugal and of Madeira, lovely as it was. It was in the interests of both combatants to have a safety valve, a place where they could carry out the intrigues of spying, and where Britons were able to share restaurants with Nazis.

None of that, of course, entered the minds of any of the Levy family, least of all Momy and his brother and sister. When they went to that park, all seemed right with the world – a planet with deathly problems from which they were shielded and cosseted. There were other things, too, of which they knew nothing: the agonies that must have engulfed Momy's father, then in his late 50s, retired unwillingly from his business and taken away from his natural environment. Momy, even now, only hints at this: 'We would be taken to the park every day because my father had nothing to do', he says. It was not difficult to read between the lines. 'Our parents would take us and then we'd go to the cafeteria there for a cup of coffee.' Plainly an enlightened couple, Mr and Mrs Levy. Children were not often allowed the luxury of tea or coffee – nor did they even want it. A glass of lemonade or orange squash was usually offered while the parents had their share of caffeine.

They enjoyed the open-air life. Particularly at home, where there was a patio – a real luxury to people brought up in a flat in Gibraltar. The big house where they lived was shared by Momy's close relatives: Isaac's bachelor brother Haim, Momy's aunt Rachel Maman and her sister-in-law Esther. When Momy went to school and his mother was out, Abraham and their sister stayed at home, looked after by these women.

It was time for one of Momy's first love affairs – with a special kind of music: 'I remember a Spanish lady who married a Gibraltarian and she put on a show and sang.' That almost could have been a chance for Momy himself to go into show business:

> She heard me sing and I took part in an exhibit of a zarzuela, my favourite Spanish music to this day. It's more than just music. I suppose you could call it the Spanish equivalent of Gilbert and Sullivan. I did two separate zarzuelas which my mother had taught me.
>
> Since the age of 8, whenever we had a rest, my mother used to sit me next to her and she'd say to me, 'Momy, come and listen to this.' Then I think, when I was 10 or 11 years old, I just wouldn't eat. My father worried about this and one of the first pieces of furniture I remember him buying was a radiogram – it was for me so that I could listen to zarzuela, but only on condition that I would eat. So I ate my lunch and my dinner and I could have my zarzuela. I still have those 78 rpm records.

Years later, Momy became the president of the Zarzuela Society in Gibraltar, an honour to add to all the others on his curriculum vitae:

> The Cervantes Centre opened here and I went to see the director. I told him, 'Look, you may not be aware of it, but here in Gibraltar, there's a lot of love for zarzuela. Let's try to promote it.' So we called a meeting and about thirty people came and decided to meet every other Tuesday in Cork's Bar, a local hostelry.

Much later in his life, as we shall see, Momy had another experience on stage, which also seemed to indicate that the stately estate agent and member of the establishment had possibly missed his vocation – when he played the rabbi (what else?) in a local version of *Fiddler on the Roof*. That, of course, was about a very different kind of Jewish life. Small it may have been (and the community in Madeira was much smaller), but Gibraltar was hardly a shtetl, although, when you come to analyse it, there *was* a lot that they had in common. The citizens were a small, compact group surrounded by a much bigger population (relatively speaking) who managed to live their lives fairly oblivious to their surroundings – which is why Momy and James plead for greater Jewish participation in local affairs. Unlike the shtetl dwellers of *Fiddler*, they have the chance and freedom to do just that. James told me:

> This is the only community in the world where you have all of Judaism under one roof. You have the very Orthodox, the Orthodox, the traditional, the liberal – all under one roof. Now, that has its challenges, but it's very fulfilling. There are tensions, big tensions, but with compromises we actually get by. Everybody compromises. People are very tolerant here. Nobody asks, 'Why didn't you go to shul on Shabbat?' So you get a wedding that everybody turns up for. You get, God forbid, a funeral, and everybody turns up.

If there were religious problems in Madeira, Momy and his brother and sister knew nothing about it. And if they did, would they have worried? The cinema, the park and the show all seemed to indicate happiness. Ask a child about all these things and he or she will reply that life is really perfect. It was, however, really the only life they knew. All of them were too young to have remembered much about Gibraltar.

And nothing interrupted their Jewish life in Madeira. They couldn't get kosher meat, but they did have chicken, and a great deal of locally caught fish. The chicken came courtesy of a Mr Moses (or Moshe) Mattana, a part-time shochet, or ritual slaughterer. For a family for whom meat was an essential part of every day living, poultry formed a compromise of sorts, and one they got to appreciate. Sadly for the members of the community who observed the dietary laws – and most did – Mr Mattana was only qualified to kill the chickens. He couldn't slaughter cattle, no matter how many people tried to persuade him to learn.

Momy, who, as we have seen, has inherited a need for red meat along with his favourite bottle of red wine, did not suffer as did the rest of his family. Momy was about 6 when he was taken ill. A doctor diagnosed a condition which he said could only be eased by a regular diet of animal flesh: 'I became very weak and the doctor ordered I change my diet.' Kosher meat was not a possibility. The doctor was not impressed. 'This boy must eat meat' – Momy remembers, to this day, the voice of the doctor making the declaration – 'If he doesn't eat meat, he is going to be seriously ill.' So that was how Momy came to eat non-kosher *treifah* meat. Three times a week, his mother and father walked him to the Savoy Hotel, where a plate of meat with tomato sauce would be awaiting him and which he ate with his father looking on: 'It was the only time in my life that I had that. I have to say it tasted very nice.' Isaac, undoubtedly an observant Jew, consulted a rabbi. There was no doubt that this was permissible. Nevertheless, one has the impression that although it was a medical necessity, a man called Solomon Levy remains not totally happy that it happened: 'Honestly, to this very day, I can see the plate of meat in front of me and my eating it.'

Jewish life was not like it had been in Gibraltar. There was no way that it could have been. But they did what they could, and what they could do was fairly remarkable. The 200 Jews formed a tiny Gibraltarian enclave. They established a small synagogue in the home of David Benaim, one of the important figures in what had been their bigger community, and services were held every day. 'It was a very big and very beautiful house', Momy remembers. As for the Levy family, they also neglected nothing that was in their power to do. Jewish life at home continued apace – to an inordinate degree, some might think.

Memories of Madeira may be sparse (at one time Momy said he only remembered going to bed, getting up, going to school and then to the park). But, as we talked, other reminiscences came back:

> There was, for instance, a Mrs Bendilt who used to come to the Yom Kippur service. I was too young to fast, so my mother prepared sandwiches for me. The lady was very distinguished and very German and she used to say to me, 'Can I share your sandwiches with you?'

Momy also remembers the amount of time the family spent listening to the wireless, as the radio was called in England in those days. All the time, thanks to their very big radio set, they had kept in touch with Britain and British life: 'To this day, I can see my parents sitting there, near the radio and listening to Winston Churchill saying, when it was all over, "This is your victory." My parents sat and cried like two little babies. Ever since then, my father virtually canonized Churchill.' And so, it must be said, did Momy, as the models of the war leader in the living room of his flat and the pictures on the wall of his own study there demonstrate.

Momy's 43-year-old son Isaac is convinced that the period his father spent in Madeira was responsible for his love and admiration for Great Britain, and for the wartime prime minister. As Isaac told me: 'He was motivated by, even as a small boy, hearing the voice of Churchill on the radio. Ever since then there has been an element of gratitude that Britain looked after Gibraltar.'

But Britain didn't immediately show its gratitude to the Gibraltarian exiles. Once the war was over, the British authorities were taking their time in arranging the exiles' departure from Madeira and the subsequent passage home. Eventually it happened. The first the family knew about it was in a telegram from a friend called Peter, a Gibraltarian who had been allowed to stay because he was an air-raid warden, living on the Rock. It said that their application to return 'will be immediately entertained' and it 'advise[d] you book passages immediately'.

Much else is a closed book to Momy these days. I asked him what his own emotions were, knowing that hostilities were over and he and his family were about to go back to Gibraltar. 'I'll be honest with you. I can't remember. I don't have that sort of memory. I do admire my friends who have those memories about this and that. But I don't – unless it was something special.' Life in Madeira was natural to this 8-year-old boy and so, it seems, was going back to Gibraltar – which the family did, once the word came from Britain that a ship was on its way to take them back to their home.

There is one thing that Momy does remember:

> When we got off the boat, we were taken in an army truck to outside the Elliot Hotel – an assembly place – and we went there because it was near the command pay office; they used to pay the soldiers there. I was very excited. Here was I, a little boy of 8, sitting on top of an open-air army truck. What could be more exciting! We got out of the truck at Governor's Lane, where we took out our luggage.

Governor's Lane was where Momy and his siblings were born and was where the family flats were. It could also be said – if you wanted to be poetic about it, but it wasn't much of a time for poetry – that that was where their hearts were, too. The Levys themselves had lived in their apartment since their marriage in 1935.

It had a terrace and, to Momy, a number of historic family moments centred around that fairly cramped area of open-air Gibraltar life: 'That's where I had my barmitzvah party. My parents put up an awning and we had about twenty boys coming to my big day. Of course, there was also a dinner at home for the family.'

It was very much a Sephardi barmitzvah:

> A rabbi from Tangiers came to teach me, a man called Shalom. A good name, that! Shalom Edery – a family that is still around in Gibraltar. The rabbi was what I would call a very modern man. He didn't even have a beard to start with and wasn't married. Later he did get married, when he went to South America. When Jews started to leave Morocco he helped them come here to Gibraltar. My uncle [Sir Joshua Hassan] helped set up a transit camp for Jewish people being taken to Morocco as a stopping-off point on the way to Israel. I think it is true to say that about half the men who have been in government in Israel had been in that Gibraltar transit camp as they moved from Morocco to their new country.

During the Second World War, the future mayor and Chief Minister had continued to work for the evacuees, who mostly wanted to get back to Gibraltar, hostilities or no hostilities. It was as though he himself had gone to Madeira or Jamaica or even London, fighting in their corners, the places where most were not as lucky as his own family, and grumbled, moaned and yearned to be allowed to go home.

Sir Joshua stayed in Gibraltar throughout the war. He was a civilian who was deemed to be essential to the Rock, as a member of the local council, and was also in the Gibraltar Defence Corps, as it was then known.

Momy had actually gone to Tangiers for his barmitzvah lessons – 'because I had aunts there – two sisters of my father were married to two gentlemen from Tangiers. And', he added with a smile, as a sort of afterthought which one can imagine was the real reason for his readiness to have the lessons, 'because there was such a beautiful beach in Tangiers. The best in Europe, I'd say. Every summer, we used to go to Tangiers anyway, spending the whole summer there. My aunts used to say I needed "a good steak for Momy to make sure he puts on weight". Well, the steaks were pretty good.' Maybe even better than the lessons: 'One of my uncles, David Edery, also taught me Torah. I still remember my barmitzvah portion by heart.'

He learned his portion of the Torah and, as nearly all barmitzvah boys do, made his father glow and his mother cry just a little in pride. But for Momy himself it wasn't going to be like other barmitzvah boys' big days: 'I said to myself, this is going to be unique.' As far as he was concerned, unique it was.

Although he had Rabbi Edery's (no relation to the uncle) teaching – or learning, as Orthodox Jews like to consider it – he had already had his share of Hebrew education and knowledge of the Torah, which for his people is much more than a collection of old Bible adventures. In those stories of what Christians would call the Old Testament, there is the fount of the wisdom that has lasted the Jews for thousands of years. Unlike the New Testament, all is not good and forgiving in the older version of the Bible. Ask an Orthodox rabbi how he could readily accept such events as the flood that led to the creation of Noah's Ark, and he is quite likely to reply, 'because it's in the Sefer

Torah' – the book of Torah, written by hand on a scroll that is read, portion by portion, in the synagogue every Shabbat and twice during the week, the same in every synagogue in the world.

That, of course, was still five years away. The exciting thing for Momy and his brother and sister was being in what seemed to them to be a new home in one of the flats, all of which had been requisitioned for use by the army – the buildings and all their furniture.

For most people, the news that soldiers were taking over their homes – the places on which the owners had lavished so much love and money, where their own ideas of comfort and style might not have been everybody's cup of Gibraltar-brand tea, but for them was everything – it was a thought that was terrible and frightening. The fears of many were totally justified. When their homes were eventually restored to them – restored in terms of bricks and mortar, but little else – owners found wallpaper torn off and replaced by graffiti, furniture smashed or seriously damaged. And with nothing from the War Office in Whitehall other than a possible letter of thanks.

'We were lucky', recalled Momy. 'They had all been requisitioned by the army, but ours had been very well looked after, fortunately, and taken over by a Major Balfour – who left a couple of his medals behind. To me, those medals were the best toys I had. I walked around the house wearing them. As a little boy, I was already wearing medals.' An historic moment if ever there were one. Anyone knowing Momy could understand that – until they think of his other toys, like his soldiers, his memorabilia.

There was no rent paid or any other kind of compensation for doing their duty and allowing their home to be used by a kind army major: 'Nothing whatsoever. The compensation was that he really looked after our place, while other people had their homes pulled down. But we started life again – at home in Gibraltar.'

Of course, Gibraltar itself was totally different from the Rock city territory of today. Now it is a comforting blend of old and new: the old full of what the guide books like to describe as 'character', the new with a kind of newness that doesn't shout its presence. Momy says of the place to which he had come: 'Actually, there were hardly any buildings at all. People were still living in Nissen huts, quite literally. Housing was just not available for most returning Gibraltarians. There was a terrible housing shortage – and there still is now; actually, there has always been one.'

He doesn't agree with me that the new buildings fit in with the old, now that those Nissen huts have long come down. As he told me, 'They're spoiling the character of Gibraltar. I'd rather they build more flats for rent and not go and live in Spain – because those who do lose their characteristic of being Gibraltarians.' Those who came back still had those characteristics, mainly through a sense of loyalty. When they returned they boosted the population to 25,000 – just 5,000 fewer than today.

It was important that the family had taken over their own old flat at Governor's Lane. Now, back home Rachel could prepare for the births of her other two children – they, too, would be born in Governor's Lane: 'My mother had five children and never did she go to hospital. She had a doctor and a midwife. The doctor lived opposite.'

Also opposite were the soldiers of what before long would become the Gibraltar Regiment. If Momy's love of the army could be precisely dated, it probably would have started then, when the 9-year-old Master Levy heard the trombones and trumpets of bandsmen in uniform: 'At that time, we had 3,000 service personnel here.' Life back home was accompanied by the sound of their bands:

> I'm crazy about military bands. My mother used to say, 'I'm not surprised. When I was giving birth to you, there was a guard

> mounting outside – to the sound of the bands.' The last Sunday of the month, they would play for the service [at the chapel]. I used to be in bed listening to the whole service with the band there. First of all there was the peal of the one bell in the chapel and then – wonderful – the sound of the bands.

(There was a certain amount of variety in those bands, who came to Gibraltar for a stay of about two-and-a-half years. They had the pick of military musicians – the ensembles of the Middlesex Regiment one year, for instance, and the Sussex Regiment the next, and so on. Eventually, the Gibraltar Defence Force, which later became the Royal Gibraltar Regiment, took over.)

'It was very much a life made to measure for the family, living in one of three flats in a block, which all belonged to the trustees of the Hebrew Poor Fund. Originally, it belonged to my mother's grandfather. When he died, he left it to the poor.' Momy has continued the association with the fund. 'Since I started to work here in 1960, I have looked after their property. I didn't charge – and I don't charge now. I look after the Methodists' fund, too – free.'

That, too, was part of his father's legacy. Momy promised Isaac that, in the cause of interfaith relations, he would never charge religious institutions for any work he did for them. Now, whenever the Church of Scotland, the Methodists or the local Roman Catholics need valuations, Momy gets the call from them, too – and they don't get the bill:

> The local Freemasons asked me to value a place for them. I had never been inside a Freemasons' temple, which is usually banned to non-Masons and I am not one of them, but I did the job free of charge because that is the thing to do. We don't have a Council of Christians and Jews here – because we, frankly, don't need one.

That was all in the future when the Levy family returned to Gibraltar. Governor's Lane was very much home. Momy recalls:

> An interesting thing is that although my father was an estate agent he never moved out of this flat. We had two bedrooms, a living room, kitchen and bathroom – and there were seven of us altogether. Some of us would go to live with my aunt or we were away at school – two of us out all the time. But it was still cramped.

And still a home: 'He [my father] never wanted to move. When we stopped having a full-time live-in maid, her room became vacant, so I made that my bedroom.' It was all due to General Franco, among whose crimes has to be added the reduction in the Levy domestic staff: 'Franco closed the frontier, so we couldn't have that luxury of a maid from Spain. But we had a Moroccan woman to come and help. So I benefitted by having that maid's room. It was right opposite the Governor's residence and the King's Chapel next to it. My window was right across from the chapel.'

Another sister and James followed to add to the Levy population. But Madeira had left its mark. There were certain legacies of the five years during which they stayed in Madeira. There was the Portuguese language, for one thing. Momy remembers:

> When I became mayor, we twinned Madeira and Gibraltar. So it was my duty to go over there to do the honours. I gave a speech in front of 200 people there. The entire council was there. My speech was translated into Portuguese. Then I spoke. When I finished, the Mayor of Madeira said, 'Momy, nineteen out of twenty.' They had found out where I had lived and where I had gone to school, all about my life in those five years we lived in Madeira. I had a chauffeur-driven car and they took me

everywhere. And they gave me fish – wrapped in foil so that I could eat it.

Only about a quarter of the Jews who had left Gibraltar at the start of the war went back there. A lot of them had gone to England and decided to stay. According to Momy, they found that Gibraltar had become a very different place: 'It was obvious when the war ended, all the problems of the world were reflected in microcosm here. My father, who had exhausted nearly all of his capital, had to start again. Eventually, things developed and then Gibraltar grew in importance. Now, of course, we punch far above our weight generally.'

Momy rarely did any punching himself – if ever. Life at home after Madeira really was good, and easy. Clearly this was regarded as an upper-class family. For one thing, they had servants, which some people brought up in England before the Second World War would not have regarded as at all strange, but by the time Field Marshal Montgomery accepted the German surrender in May 1945, this was something from the past – which shows how Gibraltar was not exactly replicating life in austerity Britain. Momy listed the servants who entered his household after the war – not boasting; it was an establishment of fact: 'We had a Spanish chauffeur, two maids and a seamstress. We used to pay the maids £15 a month. The seamstress was important for us because our clothes needed mending and we didn't just throw them away.' That was luxury, but the kind the family took for granted. But the war ended just in time, as far as the family finances were concerned. '[My father] had spent all his savings', said Momy. 'Thank God, he had his furnished flat business. We used to have maids and the chauffeur, but when we came back we were really skint.'

There were still the rents, partly from a block in City Mill Lane, one of the crevices that seem to have been carved out of the rock of

Gibraltar, which the family had owned since 1895 and which is still in their possession. 'But it wasn't enough to prevent us being otherwise skint. My uncle who had looked after it all while we were away said, "I have done my half of the business, now it's up to you."'

So Isaac, perhaps refreshed from five years away from home, possibly just determined to show that he still had the will and energy to carry on, got to work, redeveloping his properties. He knew what he wanted and instructed his architect accordingly, as Momy explained:

> I remember he [the architect] used to say to me, 'Your father, I'm his tailor. He tells me he wants a jacket this way, but I tell him where I want the pockets.' And he would tell the architect himself: 'Now, here, in this corner, I want a bedsitter. Here in this corner, I need a space. There I want two rooms and a kitchen. Here I want one room and a kitchen ... you're the architect, you prepare it.' The architect said, 'Fair enough.'

So the suit was made, bespoke, to Isaac's specifications. By the time he finished, there were about twenty-six flats. He decided to let them out furnished, connect them to services and that's how he went back into business.

Among Isaac's tenants were soldiers – this time paying rent for properties which they had to agree would be returned in the condition into which they at first moved. The military base had not been totally closed down at war's end and the War Office didn't have enough accommodation for the non-demobbed troops.

Life seemed sweet enough once the family had finished settling in to their new/old home. And that appears to have been the situation with the other Jewish 're-immigrants'. There was a Jewish club in those days,

> where people used to get together and natter. Then we had a kind of unofficial youth club that used to meet in the big hall of the Hebrew School, to which I used to go when we first got back to Gibraltar. There was also a Wizo (women's Zionist) group, which still meets. It used to be very strong and my mother would go there on Tuesdays. Nobody would go anywhere else in the community.

Momy's education, after leaving Madeira, was – like the previous collection of servants – as impressive as it could be in Gibraltar. It all had to be paid for – there was no available free schooling on the Rock at the time – which added to the necessity of moving away from being 'skint'. The life that the Levys had lived in their house on the Rua Azaranas in Madeira might suggest that 'skint' was a relative term. But Momy is adamant: 'My father didn't have a penny to his name.'

Momy first went to a small private school, run by a Mrs Teuma. She had two sisters who also used to teach. It was a primary school – very primary: the three Rs and little else. He later went to the the local St George's School. One teacher stood out above all the others there: a Miss Undery. 'She was a saint. Many years later, she decided she wanted to go to the Jewish old-age home, where she died. She wasn't Jewish. She was Protestant.'

Then he went to the Sacred Heart, run ... yes, by the Christian Brothers (although he would go to the Hebrew School in the afternoons for Jewish religious tuition). It was the old alma mater of his idol, Sir Joshua. Meanwhile, his sisters went to the convent, the building opposite Momy's office, which was close to the home and office of the Governor. The Convent now is the Governor's residence, even though there are no nuns – like the ones who taught his mother and sisters – to be seen.

Later he went to the 114-year-old Hebrew School. Momy remembers it as doing a good basic job. It had closed at the start of the war, simply because there were no Jewish children left on the Rock:

> After the war, the government did not want to give it back. They wanted it to be turned into a non-denominational school. In the end, the Jewish community did get it returned. The idea was that they would teach secular subjects in the morning, and in the afternoon there would be religious studies. Our parents had to pay for the afternoon sessions. My father and David Benaim [who was the president of the newly re-established community] battled with the authorities for nearly a year and finally we got it back.

The trouble was not so much with the Government of Gibraltar as with non-Jewish children's parents: 'The non-Jewish community really created a fuss. They said, "It's not right. We've always been together and now you're starting segregation." What I used to tell them was that they sent their children to private schools in England and paid for their education. We keep our children in Gibraltar.' Today, Momy believes that as high a figure as 99 per cent of Jewish children go to the Jewish schools. It is always difficult to guess percentages and it is easy to come up with one of this kind, but Momy has a feel for the subject and he could easily be right. He uses the same figure to establish the number of Jewish children who pass their school exams.

As we have seen, that happened largely due to Benaim and Levy, who, after a long battle, did get their way. Isaac made a speech calling on the colonial authorities to allow the school to run according to its original ethos. It was a school that was financed out of public funds, but Isaac, who sat on the committee which was set up to establish a Jewish school, set about raising money among the wealthier members of the Jewish community to prove that it could exist independently. 'It was thanks to Benaim as well as my father that we were able to re-establish that school at a time when it was potentially very difficult to organize Jewish life in Gibraltar.'

One of the problems was the feeling that perhaps the local authorities were concerned that Jewish children would have an advantage over others on the Rock. 'My father and David fought, fought and fought and eventually got it back. After all, it belonged to the Jewish community in the first place and so we had a pretty strong claim to it.'

They taught a lot of Midrash – stories based on the Talmud: 'I liked the stories. I learned how to read Hebrew, but there was no Gemarrah or Mishnah' (which are the main parts of Talmud). He went to the school at the age of 10. 'We had non-Jewish children as well as gentile teachers. They chose to go there, as parents do all over the world where there are Jewish schools, because they appreciated the Jewish values of education. It is a situation that continues today', Momy adds. Those Gentiles who appreciated the Jewish values, he maintains, included, in particular, Jehovah's Witnesses – possibly because of their traditional ultimate hope of proselytizing conversion, but that was never talked about. Nobody distributed *The Watchtower* in the school to push the Witnesses' cause. (Because a religious Jew does not mention God's name, Momy himself refuses to say the complete title of the group, calling them simply 'the Witnesses'. 'It's holy', he said.)

There are still vestiges of Momy's early boyhood around, such as the Boy Scouts. Momy was an inveterate joiner even then, so the Scouts gave him an opportunity to be a member of something that he and his parents thought worthwhile. Besides, he liked the uniform (of course): the khaki shorts and tunics, the badges and the pointed hat. He liked it better than school uniforms.

Momy was 12 when he went to the Sacred Heart, where he stayed for a year and a half. It might be thought that this institution, run by black-coated Christian Brothers, was not an ideal place for a nice Jewish boy. Isaac didn't think that, but there were changes afoot. After Momy reached 13 and had his barmitzvah, Isaac had other plans for him: to go to a school in England. It was called Carmel College.

A SCHOOL CALLED CARMEL

He was a very good footballer. He packed a strong kick and sometimes mistook his opponent's leg for the ball.

Robert Seruya

The idea came from an Orthodox rabbi who loved playing cricket: the scion of a Chassidic family who had a dream which to some inhabitants of Stamford Hill or Golders Green seemed more like a nightmare – the establishment of a Jewish public school. Not a public school in the American sense of the term, but one that taught Latin and Greek and where the boys – and originally they were just boys – were boarders who went rowing on the Thames (with an 'eight' that competed at Henley Royal Regatta) and sang the school song. They were also expected to cover their heads, eat only kosher food, say prayers from an Orthodox siddur and on Shabbat read the Torah and have a full service, complete with songs, private prayer and a message from the rabbi. In effect, a Jewish Eton or Harrow.

It was the school to which Momy went – with the number 117. Only 116 boys had started there before him. It wasn't old enough to have developed the traditions of which the other schools could boast. And, truth be told, it didn't last long enough to become one of the great British – or even great Jewish – institutions.

And yet, for a time, it was a roaring success, with young Jews from all over the world signing on to be pupils there. That was Carmel College. The inspiration behind Carmel was a charismatic, extraordinarily handsome young rabbi who would have become Chief Rabbi, had he not been quite so young – or so most observers of the Anglo-Jewish scene believe.

Inspirational? When Momy Levy went there, to be followed before long by his younger brother Abraham, the rabbi was one of the three most inspiring figures in his life: 'First came God, then my father and then Kopul Rosen.' In those early days, Rabbi Kopul Rosen's dream was transferred to his pupils like pollen to a flower. And the flowers flourished as a result – although, as we shall see, that was not everyone's opinion. Of course, there were some of those boys who were more like weeds, but the Levy boys, flown in from Gibraltar, were certainly not among them.

There was one other man at Carmel who, if not quite Kopul Rosen, was a huge influence. Dr Alexander Tobias was remarkable: 'He could tell you in 1953, without consulting any book, what time Shabbat would start on a day in 3005.'

Momy went there following in the footsteps of his friend Robert Seruya. Isaac Levy had heard from Seruya's parents that their boy had been doing well there since he joined in the very first group of students, who became part of what was undoubtedly an experiment, in 1949, so he thought it would be a good place for his son, too, in the 1950 intake.

Meeting Kopul Rosen is the first memory Momy has of his entry into Carmel College, which is perhaps why the man was to have such a huge influence on him: 'When I arrived there, I was immediately sent to the principal's study. I saw this extraordinarily impressive figure, small beard, beautifully dressed, wearing his gown, but not his mortarboard. And he said, "Welcome. I hope you'll be happy here." And, somehow, I knew I would – despite early moments of extreme homesickness.' Rosen provided immediate assurance of that happiness, despite the somewhat forbidding presence he must have offered

– in that gown, with that beard – 'because I knew he was something very special. I think I also knew even then that I would owe him everything.' It had a lot to do with his eyes, Momy thinks: 'I can see his face now. Rabbi Rosen looking up – the way he looked at me. Those eyes.'

In the Christian Brothers school, this Jewish boy had always felt 'quite at home'. But now it was an entirely new experience. At Carmel, there were non-Jewish teachers and they were the ones who were now the minority. For a Jewish boy brought up in an extremely Jewish home with an Orthodox Jewish family, there was tremendous psychological effect there.

'There was Mr Warner who tried to teach me Latin and Greek. And I felt really that this was a taste of university, despite the fact that I wasn't a brilliant student and wouldn't eventually go to university, but I felt as if I were there under Mr Warner.'

Some changes were on the way, even that early on in the school's history. And they left a legacy.

> There was a teacher at Carmel who actually came from Gibraltar. One day, he asked Rabbi Rosen if he could introduce some non-Jewish boys to the school. The rabbi said he could – but they would have to realize it was a Jewish school and would be expected to take part in the Jewish religious activities. One of them became a doctor who now lives in Marbella. He would stop me in the street and he says to me, 'Momy, shall we sing *Zemirot* (the Sabbath table hymns)?' Kopul Rosen treated them all alike.

Education there was not just the usual set subjects, but also a sense of history that was a living thing, a chance to experience both the majesty of and the glories of the Oxfordshire countryside where Carmel was situated. Ask Momy which of the many things he enjoyed most there, and he'll say the introduction to classical music, sitting in the principal's study and listening to records that Rabbi Rosen himself played on his turntable, dissecting and analysing every piece to which he encouraged the boys to listen. When Rosen saw that the music was appreciated, a smile would engulf his face, his small, elegant beard twitching slightly in satisfaction.

The head probably enjoyed the music as much as when he stood at the crease with a bat firmly in his grip and the hope in his mind that he might score the most runs of the day. It was an image fondly picked up by the *Jewish Chronicle* when this strange amalgam of religion and secular thought advertised for its first students. 'The best of English schools combine with the best of Judaism' was what the sales campaign boasted.

The idea of a Jewish boarding school in Britain was not unknown. There had been other attempts in earlier times. A few boys boarding with an austere gentleman and his wife was one of the ideas that took off and broke down throughout the Victorian era before the mass immigration from Eastern Europe at the turn of the twentieth century – particularly if the gentleman had a healthy growth of whiskers and his wife a severe look on her face, a drab black dress up to her neck and a bosom giving it, shall we say, a certain structure. More recently, there had been a school near Brighton called Whittingham College – Whittingham was the name of the estate of (Arthur) Lord Balfour, a kind of tribute to the man who made his famous 'Declaration', offering the thought that His Majesty's Government looked with favour at the idea of a Jewish homeland. It was run by a Mr Halevy and for a time the more wealthy Jewish families in Britain thought it offered their sons the chance to become good English gentlemen and eat just kosher food and celebrate the Jewish holydays.

The more wealthy Jews had another choice: Polack's House at Clifton College, near Bristol, where the same facilities were offered, but in the midst of one of the leading British public schools.

And then came Carmel, an altogether more ambitious undertaking, situated in what had been a beautiful old house, complete with a beautiful old staircase, in Oxfordshire. It would move to another big house to which would later be added purpose-built glass buildings donated by Jewish businessmen such as the famous Sir Isaac Wolfson, head of Great Universal Stores and President of the United Synagogue, Anglo-Jewry's principal 'modern Orthodox' organization. Carmel was in an area which quite a few years later would conjure up an entirely different meaning – it was called Greenham Common.

Carmel was like none of the other establishments – as much as anything because in addition to what in the late 1940s and early 1950s might have been considered (although the term was then unknown) state-of-the-art facilities, it had that one unique feature named Kopul Rosen.

Dr Yaacov Kopul Rosen rarely used the name Yaacov, and his close family and friends called him 'Kop', which – since that is Yiddish for 'head' – was probably all the more appropriate. (The first and other two initials actually live on in the acronym for a leading religious educational establishment which was started by his son, the late Rabbi Michael Rosen, in London and is now based in Israel, called Yakar.) His Chassidic background dictated that he would probably go into the rabbinate, although he was never going to be the kind of rabbi that would have been expected. This was a man so immersed in both Judaism and British culture that heading an institution such as Carmel was practically inevitable. The latter was always extraordinarily important to him, but he never lost his total belief in traditional – if not ultra-Orthodox – Judaism. Indeed, his rabbinical training was at the world-famous Yeshiva etz Chaim in London and what was always considered the pre-Holocaust citadel of Talmudic learning, the Mir Yeshiva in Lithuania.

He lived only until he was 48, but in those years he chalked up an amazing litany of achievements and offices. At the age of 25, in 1938, he was appointed rabbi of the Higher Crumpsall Synagogue, one of the leading Jewish prayer centres in Manchester, then as now a city with the second-largest Jewish community in Britain. In 1942, he was made Communal Rabbi of Glasgow. Then, in 1944, he was appointed principal rabbi of the Federation of Synagogues, an outpost of the still-immigrant generation of Jews for whom London's United Synagogue was considered 'too English'. Knowing Rosen's passion for all that was best in Britain, this was an ironical situation.

It was in 1948, the year that Israel Brodie succeeded the dynamic, controversial Joseph Herman Hertz as Chief Rabbi, that Rosen decided to leave the rabbinate in its traditional role. Some saw it as pique at being denied Hertz's job, although most felt that, being only 35, he would have another chance the next time the post became vacant. But he would never have that opportunity. In 1962, leukaemia won a battle he thought he could overcome – after all, Menachem Meir Schneersohn, the Lubavitcher 'rebbe' whom he consulted in New York (a demonstration of his continual loyalty to his Chassidic roots) said that he would. He died, leaving his wife, Bella (herself a feature of Carmel), a baby daughter, and three sons – all of whom became rabbis, and one, Jeremy, succeeding his father as the school's principal.

There was, however, another fight that he did win: the establishment in the year he didn't get the Chief Rabbinate of something he considered more important – Carmel. After all, he had gone around the country talking about the 'crisis' in Jewish education that he thought he could help overcome with his new school.

To Momy, the combination of Kopul Rosen with God – 'without him, I wouldn't be here', which you could say for his father, too – is anything but flippant. And it crossed the barriers between scholastic prowess and personality. Listening to Mr Levy you could be forgiven for thinking that Rosen's personality came first: 'He was very handsome, very elegant. And the way I dress I owe to him.' So now we know. 'In appearance, every day was Shabbat for him. He dressed impeccably.'

And more: 'He used to go and watch us play football.' (A video released several years ago by the school showed him making signs of desperation as the Carmel team plainly did not play the way he would have liked. The expression on his face and the hand clutching his forehead spoke a Hebrew book.) 'He also watched our attempts at basketball. And even then, no jeans or anything formal. He wore what for other people would be their best suit.'

For Momy, Rosen's musical instruction made the biggest impression:

> When I came to Carmel in September 1950, I didn't have the slightest idea what classical music was. And there were two or three other boys with whom after lunch, from Monday to Thursday, I would go to his study and for a quarter of an hour or so, he'd play parts of a symphony or ballet music, like a suite from *Swan Lake*. He'd put on a record and we'd go from Mozart to Beethoven. Then he would take us to concerts – by the LSO [London Symphony Orchestra] and the Royal Philharmonic. He'd get us special tickets so that we could go and hear them in London. If there was a soloist he particularly admired, a violinist or a pianist, he would make sure we would be there to hear them. Thanks to him I now love classical music.

In fact, it went further than that: 'I went on my own to see the Halle Orchestra.' Momy would take trips to the Royal Albert Hall, or the Royal Festival Hall – which itself was an echo of Carmel and Kopul Rosen: 'He took us there for the opening of the Festival of Britain in 1951.' Momy got to love the theatre, too, which in later years would hold him in good stead. It was his favourite recreation when he took his first job in London – when he could afford it.

But the most significant memory for most people was Kopul's gift of the gab. Momy said: 'When he spoke – even to a rowdy crowd of boys – you could hear a pin drop.'

He took up the connection of his old school principal with the deity once more – in fact, Momy constantly links the two: 'God did a lot for me, in having been Kopul Rosen's pupil.'

Rosen was at first buried in the grounds of the second building that Carmel took over, the Mansion House near Wallingford in Oxfordshire. But when the school eventually closed in 1996, his remains were taken to Jerusalem, where his three sons then lived.

Knowing Momy as we do by now, one of the strange discoveries is that when it came to talking to Kopul Rosen, he was strangely shy. Even remembering his mentor seems to show a different Momy. Maybe it is the awe in which Rosen is still held by the former Mayor of Gibraltar. I asked him if he talked to Rosen about Israel.

> I was scared to talk to him about anything – because I didn't want to put my foot in it. That was why, when he asked me to do anything, I would never say No. I tried to hide what I felt by doing something very different. There was a fancy dress competition. There was Abraham and my close Gibraltar friend Robert Seruya. Because that was coming up, on a trip to London, I hired three ape suits. They were really perfect. There was a big hall in the original house, which was close to the town of Newbury. It had a big staircase where only certain people were allowed. It had magnificent bannisters. So the three of us, me, Abraham and Robert, dressed as apes and we slid down the bannisters which we were forbidden to use and someone called out, 'The saviours of Gibraltar'.

We don't know what Dr Rosen thought of that. But perhaps Winston Churchill would have taken it as confirmation of his faith in the Rock's British future.

Before long, the school had to move from its magnificent old building. The American Air Force was about to take over Greenham Common to establish its base – the one that became the centre for the cruise missiles against which, for two years, a group of women demonstrated day in, day out, camping on the site. It wasn't like that when Carmel College was there.

Indeed, as far as Momy was concerned, life was ready to change tremendously. For one thing, he would no longer be able to conduct himself on Saturdays in a very un-Sabbath-like way: 'Very often, on Shabbat, I'd sneak away, actually run away from school – to watch [the then best-known jockey in the country] Gordon Richards from a distance, racing at Newbury. We used to watch all the races.'

But it all ended in 1952. The school moved to its new Wallingford address, Mongewell Park. If he couldn't watch the horse racing, the rowers of Carmel were another thing: 'We were right next to the Thames and seeing the boats was wonderful. We used to watch the Oxford Boat Race crews practising.' So no guesses as to which side the Carmel boys supported – although they were not allowed to watch the boat race on the primitive black-and-white television that was available. The race was always on a Saturday, and Shabbat rules would have prohibited watching it. Certainly, Rabbi Kopul Rosen, modern and using the latest educational techniques though he was, would not have allowed anything that contravened the Sabbath rules.

But Momy does remember this about him:

> He was a religious man, but he wasn't an extremist. He would keep his faith to the letter but he would sometimes express things which some people thought were a bit liberal. For example, he wasn't very particular about kosher wines. He said, 'I don't drink it myself, but if you know people who don't bother, I don't think it matters that much.'

That was a symptom of the times. At Jewish weddings and other so-called 'supervised functions', there would be cards on the tables stating that the supervising authority was not responsible for the kashrut of the wines being served. Now, the question would simply not arise. If the caterer failed to have kosher drinks on the table, he would lose his licence and, along with it, his customers.

Accommodation in those days was not exactly palatial. Lessons in those early days, while plans for elaborate extensions were being put into practice, were held in a large temporary hut – similar to the kind that children in state schools in those early post-war days often had to tolerate while bomb damage was being cleared up – but Momy says it never worried him: 'Accommodation didn't bother us. The atmosphere was so nice, so satisfying.'

There was even school work to do there:

> I was the only one there doing A-level Spanish. The others were doing A-Level French – which wasn't as much of a swiz as you might think. The problem was not the language, but the literature. So I needed tuition and three times a week I'd take a bus to Oxford to a tutor. I'll never forget his name, Alan Deyermond. He was very English, very lah-de-dah, but of course, I seriously respected him. But it wasn't just the literature. When it came to the exam itself, I had to do the oral – which I have to admit I didn't find difficult.

If he had, it would have had spectacular repercussions. He had to go to another school for the exam: 'Strange boys with strange uniforms – strange, because they were not the Carmel clothes. I'll never forget the examiner and his first question to me. He said to me, in Spanish: "If you had a puncture in your bicycle tyre, how would you fix it, son?" I knew nothing about inner tubes.' What Momy said was equally unexpected and, you might think, disrespectful and extraordinarily patronizing: 'I just told him the truth. I said, "If I had a puncture in my bicycle, I would ask my father's chauffeur to fix it."' Not the best thing for a boy to say. The comments that come to mind ought not to find a place here. 'What the hell!' the examiner said. 'Where the hell have you come from?' Most people would probably think that it was simply a matter of Momy sounding rude and certainly acting the show-off. He, though, says:

> I think he was upset because my Spanish was better than his was. I answered him by saying that I'm from Gibraltar, but I've now just come back from school. We spent half an hour talking about Gibraltar – in Spanish ... and most of the rest of the time, we talked about the apes. By mentioning the chauffeur I wasn't trying to take the mickey out of him – although I wouldn't do it now – I simply never in my life had had a puncture in one of the bicycles I owned. If I had, I really would have taken the wheel off and given it to the chauffeur and he would have fixed it for me. He wanted me to talk about using the inner tube and the other things you used.

Plainly, Momy didn't know – and doesn't know now – very much about mending a cycle puncture. It is also easy to believe that he had no desire to extend his knowledge of the world by learning more.

Looking back on it now, Momy doesn't think the answers he gave annoyed the examiner, but I have, shall we say, somewhat different views. 'He was just surprised because all the other students mostly spoke in English and for me the natural language was Spanish. And he only wanted to hear proper Spanish' – which, it seems, Momy was speaking.

He learnt French, too:

> We had a master from Manchester, Emil Schlesinger. I had to give him a speech before he left the school. I'll never forget this. We

> were meant to be presenting him with a briefcase, which didn't arrive on time. So we made up a parcel and I gave him my speech in French and then presented him with the parcel. He was kind about it and seemed to understand.

Another teacher was a Catholic priest, Father Kenneth Cox. While he was at Carmel, he converted to Judaism and became an intriguing figure in Anglo-Jewish society, frequently appearing in the pages of the *Jewish Chronicle* under the name of Abraham Carmel, a more Jewish name than Kenneth Cox and, no doubt, by way of tribute to his employers and his principal.

It helped Momy, he said, in his own efforts to promote the cross-religious relations on which he has worked in Gibraltar. As he told me:

> Look, I don't know quotations from the Bible, but I know that when God said to Abraham, go and sacrifice your son, the one you love, Isaac, he also loved his other son, Ishmael. Kopul Rosen used to say, 'If I can get one boy who comes here who is not religious to be observant the way he should be, I am quite happy.'

Different standards of Judaism didn't bother Momy nearly so much:

> I remember the first Israeli I ever met, a fellow student at Carmel named Benny Schalit. He was not at all religious. I asked him why the Israelis were so proud. I couldn't understand it. When I went to Israel the first time, I understood it. But he couldn't understand us and the way we followed Judaism. He used to say, 'You're mad not to ride or turn on lights on Shabbat.'

There was good reason for Momy to like a man called Philip Refson rather more:

> His grandfather owned the Essoldo cinema chain. Essoldo was a name made from those of his three children, Esther, Solomon and

> Dorothy. There was an Essoldo in Maidenhead, which was very near Carmel College. Once a year, they would treat us to a film there, taking us by coach to the cinema.
>
> And afterwards, he would bring kosher salt beef or tongue from London and he would give us a nice meal. So it was nice going to Maidenhead, if only for our kosher meal once a year.'

Not that Carmel wasn't strictly kosher, indeed it was, but this had an air of luxury about it.

By that time, Carmel had moved to Wallingford and Momy had become a prefect. Dr Rosen's sons were pupils then, and were subject to the Solomon Levy disciplinal treatment: 'Michael [Mickey] Rosen was a good boy. Jeremy [who was to follow his father and become Carmel's principal] was a very naughty boy. I used to twist his ear' – which should be seen perhaps more as an early rehearsal for power in Gibraltar than a real indication of the Kopul heir's behaviour in class.

Momy was the prefect in charge of the prep school, which somewhat limited his powers for punishment. One of the duties he had to accept was to read the mail that came to boys who found it difficult putting the words together: 'Sometimes, I would get a parcel for one of the pupils which was very sticky. His parents had sent a chicken in the post.' Momy makes clear that he was anything but the Carmel censor: 'I just read the envelopes and distributed the mail', he explained. 'But it was difficult to avoid what was in that soggy parcel with the chicken.'

The prep school was in another building with its separate, individual dining room, which may have been the reason for a boy needing to get a chicken in the post. The poor, embarrassed (and embarrassed he surely was) boy plainly had a traditional Yiddishe Mama who thought her little boy wasn't going to get enough to eat in that prep school restaurant. Momy still feels loyal enough to say that the mother's worries were unnecessary. 'The food was plain, but it was very good', he now remembers. 'Very good for a boy at school. Sometimes, there was not enough. But nobody ever starved.' So it wasn't quite like the old joke, 'the food was terrible, like poison – and she served such small portions'. Momy continued:

> It would be very English – including roast beef, of course. We had lots of meatballs. We'd always have a light supper. Shabbat was better than the other days of the week. We used to get fish, chicken and a beautiful dessert. Oh yes – and there was this wonderful stew, which I loved.
>
> At first, I didn't really like English food which, in those days of course, was always being maligned by foodies. But I got used to it. And when a young boy is hungry, he'll eat anything. When I used to be about to go home, I used to say to my mother, 'Mummy, please give me some proper food' – and I'd list all the things I wanted. I'd give her a menu. I still like, for instance, the Spanish dish, pastelitos de patata, a round little pasta-type dish which was potato stuffed with meat. One of my favourites, which I most definitely did not get at Carmel.

He didn't argue with other meals: 'Breakfast was cornflakes, toast and sometimes scrambled eggs, sometimes cheese. On Shabbat, they only gave us biscuits and coffee until halfway through the service, as was traditional, when we used to be given a proper breakfast.'

Some people judge their school experiences by the games they played, the teachers who were either brilliant or appalling, the friends they made, the fights with those who became friends after starting out as enemies, the enemies who would never be friends, the homework which added so much stress, the punishments they tried to avoid. To Momy, being incarcerated in what was at first a strange community which would later seem like family, food took on a considerable importance. Indeed, to him food became a lifelong fascination – not quite as important as fashion, although it is probably a debatable competition. In short, Momy became fascinated by food – that which he had, and that which he hadn't sampled: 'The first time I went to England, I met two boys who were vegetarians. I didn't know it existed and I said to myself, "Vegetarian and kosher. What could anyone ask for?"' He still can't understand it. 'I was astounded. All they ate was vegetables – and I'm a carnivore. I mean, I just can't do without meat.' He had made that point before. 'If I could eat it three times a day, when I go to Israel, they have so much we don't have here – like the hind quarters, which gives me a chance to try things like fillet steak. I've done that in New York, too.' Not that he would leave Gibraltar – under any circumstances.

The public school ethos ran throughout Carmel – the main academic centre and the one for the young boys in the prep school. The house system was fairly strictly observed – it was, after all, the backbone of Eton, Harrow and Winchester. But it was also a very Jewish establishment. That being so, the houses provided a good opportunity for the people who donated money to the school to be remembered. Instead of the more traditional brass plaque, donors had the houses named after them – one a Mr Alexander, the other called Gilbert. Momy was in Gilbert House.

It has to be admitted that the houses were not really as important as they were in the longer-established public schools. Housemasters were not quite as much in loco parentis as in the other institutions. 'It was mainly for sports purposes', Momy says. 'We were in dormitories that had nothing to do with houses.' And they struck up friendships and selected the people with whom they would keep in contact. It was hardly surprising that Momy shared a study with his fellow Gibraltarian Robert Seruya. They were together throughout the three years they spent at Wallingford.

The name Seruya is very important in Jewish Gibraltar. Not only is it famous for the perfume shops run by Robert, but it is also well known because of Robert's cousin, Solomon: 'He used to be a politician here and became Minister of Tourism. Then he decided to go to Israel. So he spent six months in Israel and six in Gibraltar. Once he settled in to life in the Jewish State, he was appointed its ambassador to the Philippines. So you had a Gibraltarian serving as ambassador from Israel to the Philippines.' That is also part of the Gibraltar story. It is safe to say that while Momy Levy became very much part of Carmel College and the quasi-public school system, nothing was ever going to reduce the impact of the Rock, its history and its contemporary story on his life.

As for Solomon Seruya, Momy says, 'I wouldn't say he is pro-Spanish, but he is all for Spain having good relations with Gibraltar. They used to brand him as anti-British. He wanted what was called "Regional Co-operation" which was wrongly interpreted as handing Gibraltar to Spain.'

They didn't debate Gibraltar at Carmel, which maintained its total commitment to Britain – and, of course, to Israel. In those days, no one talked of dichotomies or dual nationality. To Kopul Rosen, that amounted to his mantra that it stood for being good Britons and good Jews.

There was one Israeli teacher at the school who also helped that idea along: 'His name was Gurtner and he was rather embarrassed by his Israeli accent.' What was probably difficult for an Israeli to grasp was this synthesis of a school that was so obviously Jewish and working so hard to be accepted as a British institution at the same time.

Football was the national game and Momy, who believed in playing the game in all spheres of Carmel life, treated soccer precisely the same way – which is partly why he played in the first eleven, competing with other schools: 'And you know what, most of the time, we won.'

But he wasn't one of the boys in the attack line-up: 'I used to play left half – Robert was centre forward. My father used to kid me when I was in the team. I wrote a letter once saying, "They [the opposing team] almost scored and I saved it by a header." My father liked that.'

The games were not restricted to playing against other public schools: 'Once we played the Mary Hare School, which was for deaf and dumb boys and was situated near Wallingford. They were very good footballers. And, of course [of course!] we had a cricket team. We used to play against Oxford University.' That sounded pretty impressive. And then he added: 'Oxford University Jewish Students.' Among their team was the man who became Senior Jewish Chaplain to the Forces as well as a judge and a barrister, the Revd Malcolm Weisman. 'He was a good player', Momy recalled. 'He played – and I was the umpire.' Many years later, Malcolm Weisman, as minister to the small communities, and Momy would meet together – without the younger Mr Levy making the decisions.

What was interesting about the synthesis between religion and secular life was the way the two things came together. Sometimes even on that sports field. Kopul Rosen may, as Momy said, have worn his best suit (in a film made at the time, he was shown watching football and wearing a coat over that suit – which, as he held his head in despair, made him look all the more like a professional football manager who saw the sack on the way; on the other hand, nobody would have dared sack the rabbi), but he had his skullcap *kippah* firmly fixed – and that was in the days before this item of headgear was connected with what would previously have been thought of as a woman's hairclip. He was not the only one who combined the two aspects of Jewish life. There was, for instance, an Israeli boy called Weinberger: 'He's a very successful lawyer now. He was a very *frum* (religious) boy. And he used to take a little Gemarrah with him when he was playing cricket. When we didn't have to bat, he'd wait at the other end to see if he had to run – if not, he carried on studying his Gemarrah.' Maybe that had something to do with the school's record at the wicket: 'We played against all sorts of schools – certainly not just Jewish schools. At football, we nearly always won. At cricket, we usually lost.' (There might be something in the blood about that – it is said that, proportionately, more middle-aged Jewish men are football supporters than are Gentiles of their age and gender.)

It wasn't just sport that figured in school activities. Music did too – and not just the kind that Kopul Rosen played on his turntable. 'There was a boy called Klein. I used to call him "the genius". He played his violin so well, he, as we say in Spanish, used to eat it. For five years, I, too, learned to play the violin, but I didn't eat it. I've never forgiven myself for giving it up when I left school.'

Carmel was clearly a huge influence on the future Mayor of Gibraltar. It goes without saying that Kopul Rosen was the biggest influence of all. Robert Seruya, who shared so much of Momy's life at the school, from travelling to and from Gibraltar together to working and playing together there, shows to this day the same enthusiasm: 'Oh, absolutely. He had a great influence on all the young students who passed through his hands and his school. And, you know, we all aspired to be that sort of person ourselves. He was a giant in the Jewish world and in the non-Jewish world, too.'

That did not mean that all Rosen's dreams for his school came true. As Seruya put it:

> Perhaps Carmel College didn't produce the sort of Jew that he wanted to create – a man who would stand high in the Jewish world, in the Jewish academic world as well as in the non-Jewish world. Unfortunately, he did not manage to create that sort of person that he was himself – and it has to be said that Momy and I were not the best examples of these two aspects.

But there was an exception, of course – Momy's brother, Abraham, who was to become spiritual leader of the Spanish and Portuguese congregation in London, in effect the British Sephardi Chief Rabbi: 'When he came to the school, two years after me, Rabbi Rosen asked if any of the boys wanted to be rabbis. Abraham put up his hand straight away – and he never wanted to be anything else. I remember when he was 6 years old, he used to stand up in bed at home and give a sermon.' Fortunately, those exercises in sermonizing got better.

Abraham was warmly welcomed to Carmel. The principal wrote to Isaac: 'I look forward to welcoming your second son. Solomon [is] a fine boy and a credit to his family. I would be happy to welcome his brother. As an indication of this feeling and in appreciation of stating your financial position, I am prepared to reduce the fee suggested to £400 per annum if the two brothers come to school.'

From Carmel, Abraham went to Jews' College and then into the rabbinate. That, too, could be put down to Kopul Rosen and the 'family school'. As Momy says about his younger brother, 'From then on, he'd come to Gibraltar for his holidays, but his life would be in London'.

As we have already seen, James did not follow his two older brothers to Carmel. Momy explained: 'You see, my father was going to send him, but our local rabbi Emanuel Pacifici stopped my father. He said it wasn't going to be *frum* enough. People in Gibraltar were just starting to be more *frum* and he recommended that James shouldn't go there.' There could have been another reason, which is extraordinarily ironical: he was such a brilliant student that his father thought he would benefit from remaining with the Christian Brothers – despite the obvious advantages that his Jewish Brothers had.

Unlike Momy, Robert Seruya doesn't see the sun shining from every Rosen orifice. Sometimes the rabbi seemed a little too frank: 'I think that Kopul perhaps taught us things that we both mention sometimes even today – things that we could not possibly understand at the age of 16 or even 18.' He didn't elaborate.

> We used to come back home on holidays, flying home together in one of those eight-hour Dakota journeys. We'd fly in those things and feel pretty bad.
>
> But not quite as bad as at school when we were small and we used to get pretty homesick and we would go into the cloakroom at school and there we would have our little cry and some master would come in – I think it was a Mr Roston, I forget now, possibly Mr Stamler. He would come there nearly every afternoon, find us there, take us to his study and give us some chocolates to try to cheer us up. And that would work miracles. But it took us quite a while.

Being at school for the holidays, as sometimes happened, particularly at half-term, wasn't easy either, says Momy:

> I remember I was at Carmel College. Half-term came along and parents would go up to their children and say something like, 'Hello, son, how are you? Nice to see you. Go over there to talk to your housemaster.' On the rare occasions when my parents were able to come, they hugged us, they kissed, and people looked as if we had come from another world. Well, we decided the others were British and we had Latin blood. Jewish, but the blood got a bit Latinized.

Today, that blood is restricted, he says, to being 'bloody annoyed'. But not all the time. This is a quiet, restrained, fun-loving man. Unless he gets 'bloody annoyed'. Then, he changes like Dr Jekyll to Mr Hyde: 'I start to shout in Spanish. I admire the English. They are quiet and don't get worked up like we do.' I pointed out that he plainly had not met a bad-tempered Englishman in a pub.

Then there were those trips home for the holidays. Saruya recalled: 'I used to spend a lot of time in Momy's home in Governor's Lane, where, in fact, James Levy now lives, opposite the house where their parents lived on the top floor. I think I would be there, on average, every other day. We were that close.'

That homesickness was not a secret kept from their parents, either. Their more serious activities included the inevitable Latin lessons: 'We were not too keen on that sort of thing, Momy and I think we would spend our time writing letters home, between Latin lessons that we couldn't follow too well.' The way Robert Seruya said that made it sound rather like an understatement.

Even before Momy wore a tailored suit, waistcoat and a bowler hat, in December 1950 he was already taking up public speaking – and public answering. Sir Isaac Wolfson had just visited and made a speech, to which Momy was deputed to reply: 'Sir Isaac talked about the need for Jews to maintain their good name.' I said, 'Very true.' You can be sure that the man who was a household name in his community must have appreciated Momy Levy's pompous approval.

Momy had not been a particularly brilliant pupil, to say the least, when he first arrived at Carmel. It did concern him, although he hadn't really been aware of any inadequacies when he was first introduced to his housemaster and the other teachers, all of whom put the fear of the Gibraltar and Carmel God in him – which was nothing compared with the first meeting with the (later to be) saintly Rabbi Dr Yaacov Kopul Rosen.

He was quickly consigned back to reality, as far as his own ability was concerned. There was the background of his education in Gibraltar and Madeira, which hardly compared with what was about to be offered at this much more prestigious establishment, to say nothing of the pre-Carmel school training of his fellow pupils. In Jewish religious education, he might have thought he would excel. His teachers at the

Gibraltar school could have specialized in those Mishnah lessons, but they didn't manage to break through the Levy brain barrier – at least, not sufficiently to put him on an equal standing with the others at his new school. So, he said, 'I realized I was behind in my studies and I started to really work.'

The young Momy wouldn't have liked to be called a mummy's boy, but before the Kopul Rosen infusion took root, all he could think of was being away from his parents, and everybody and everything he knew, for the first time: 'I used to go to a certain tree, and under it I would stand and cry my eyes out.' He didn't exactly telephone his parents and say 'Come and get me', but he did get as far as saying, 'I'm not happy here.' That was not good news to the older Levys, for whom their children represented the glories of life. But they didn't succumb to the unsaid appeals.

Momy had felt the full impact of what he believed his next five years would be when sitting on the Dakota aircraft that was going to take him to England that very fateful day in September 1950. It was a feeling of an agony being prolonged – almost as prisoners in the days of capital punishment may have prayed for it all to be quickly over with as they mounted the scaffold, knowing there was no hope. Once he was on that plane and the seat belt tightened, young 14-year-old Momy knew that all was lost. The journey didn't help – all eight hours of it: 'We flew from Gibraltar to Madrid where we had to refuel. Then it was Madrid to Bordeaux, refuelling again and then to Northolt, from which I had to get the bus to what was not quite the BEA terminal in Cromwell Road, the continuation of Kensington High Street.

This all indicates how flying has changed. Cromwell Road would eventually become the site of a terminal, in the days before everything was handled at Heathrow. But 'it was just a waiting room in those days'. And Heathrow had hardly been thought of, which was why the much smaller Northolt was the main London 'hub'.

He was met at Cromwell Road by Merita Levy, the daughter of one of his father's cousins: 'She took me to Paddington Station. She put me on the train at Paddington, where there were two other boys making the same journey.' This did not put his mind at rest; rather, he became aware of another potential problem – he realized he would be sleeping in a dormitory with five others. They talked about their expectations and fears, but the sleeping arrangements kept coming up in conversation – and the thoughts of how difficult it was going to be for young fellows who had been used to having rooms of their own. Momy saw it from his own perspective: 'And I was very worried. I had had this thing since I was very very young – I couldn't sleep in the dark. I need to be able to see some light before I go to sleep or if I awake in the night.' It became one of those obsessions that cloud everything else. Throughout that train journey, and as he entered the portals of Carmel for the first time, it was all he could think of – until he actually got to the dormitory itself. 'I needn't have worried', he says now. 'I was the first to arrive, so I managed to get the bed closest to the door to the corridor – where, underneath the door, I could see a bit of light.'

This wasn't the only development in Momy's new life. It was at Carmel, in 1950, that he heard he had a new baby brother. James had just been born: 'I always wanted to have a baby in the house. But I was sent to Carmel College in Britain and one day I was in assembly when I got a telegram from my father, "MAZELTOV, YOU NOW HAVE A NEW BROTHER." And because I was at Carmel, I wasn't able to be present and at home.' Meanwhile, Mrs Bella Rosen, the wife of the principal, sent a telegram to Gibraltar: 'HEARTIEST CONGRATULATIONS ON THE BIRTH OF YOUR SON. TO ISAAC LEVY AND FAMILY.' Momy recalls being disappointed: 'I remember I used to say to my friends, "I'd love to see a circumcision at home." [Bloodthirsty, I suppose you could call it, but that wasn't Momy's motive.] But then the telegram comes along that I had a new brother. I said, "Oh dear, I'm going to miss the *brit milah* [the circumcision]."'

He had to cope with people who would be able to hear him. Momy knew he talked in his sleep. He was concerned about the ribbing he would get from his room-mates – not about what they heard coming from his lips. There was no risk of security leaks. As he explained to me: 'I used to think in Spanish. So when I dreamt I did so in Spanish. I always knew that. But talking in my sleep?' One morning, after a particularly active night's imagination, he got the answer: 'One of my new friends said, "Look, we don't mind you giving a speech, but please speak to us in English – so that we can listen to what you're saying."' It would no longer be a problem, if, by any strange chance, he was sleeping in the same room of that friend Robert Seruya – now, like Momy, a septuagenarian: 'Now I think in English. I don't think – or talk in my sleep – in Spanish.'

Momy didn't realize how things would change for him. Whether at Greenham Common or Wallingford, the school wanted to be thought of as a second home, and Momy certainly did think of it like that. In a way, it didn't matter where the school was situated. The Carmel location was very important to the then young boys and growing men, because it represented the memories they took with them. And it is clearly why Momy talks about that aspect of his old school so much. The buildings don't have the resonance of Rabbi Kopul Rosen, but they still come to mind when he talks about what was one of the vital times in his life. All in all, he preferred the buildings at Greenham Common, even though they didn't include either a synagogue or a gymnasium: 'But it was a beautiful mansion, with a marvellous, big, very wide wooden staircase. As you went up the staircase, the first thing you would pass would be Rabbi Rosen's flat. Above that were all the dormitories.'

The disappointment for small new boys was that they were not allowed to use that staircase – 'because it did lead to the Rosens' flat'.

The only time Momy did use it in those early days was when the three Gibraltarians made a stand on behalf of their country – or at least a slide, dressed as those apes sliding down the banisters. 'Recently', Momy recalled for me, 'Robert asked me, "Are you still the ape you were when you came down that staircase?"' More than most would be. Solomon Levy gives the impression that he would still thoroughly enjoy putting on a monkey suit and looking for a banister to slide down.

The monkey outfit was not the only guise Momy adopted at Carmel. A letter from the school to his parents declared: 'I feel I must mention to you how good Momy was in the fancy dress [concert]. He came as a gollywog and [was] really excellent. He deserves first prize.' Not exactly pioneers in political correctness, those teachers at Carmel.

Mongewell Park at Wallingford was a different sort of environment, although the rules and the newly established 'traditions' (if traditions can be newly established) remained the same. Momy remembers it as just a big house in those days. 'But there were the extra glass-fronted buildings, which started to go up after I left in 1955.'

His own facilities at Mongewell Park were nothing to write home about – but, of course, he did: 'I had a so-called study. Actually, it was a hut.'

The school has long been closed, but the incredibly stylish synagogue – not just a collection of seats and a cupboard in which to store the Torah scrolls that is so often the case in communal premises – is now a listed building and has been used for countless movies. It represented the House of Commons in the film based on the not always accurate Margaret Thatcher story, *The Iron Lady*.

Even in the days before the new building with that beautiful new synagogue was built, the services were impressive. They had all of what became known in Britain as the statutory prayers, and hymns were retained and the rituals of what was generally accepted as United Synagogue 'Modern Orthodox' practice were carried out to the letter. Needless to say, the Torah readings on the 'right' week were held as in any other synagogues in the world.

It wasn't easy for him. A Sephardi, he had to learn to follow the school's Ashkenazi ritual – which also included the readings of the Torah and the Prophets, the Haftorah which followed. It may not have been easy, but he did it, thanks to a contemporary Carmel student named John Fisher:

> After a while I said to him, 'John, teach me the Ashkenazi way', which he did.
>
> Rabbi Rosen used to call out, 'Right, I want volunteers for *layning*', which is the Torah reading. I used to keep quiet, but after then I was told 'volunteer'. To this day, I think of that time and I can honestly say I still see the rabbi's face when I see that portion which I read for the first time in Ashkenazi style at Carmel.

Nobody ever called Mrs Bella Rosen an iron lady. Amazingly, she was able to combine the duties of being a wife and looking after the elegant private flat (which the boys were not allowed to approach) with those of being a mother figure for the 300-odd students who had come from all over the world: Europe, America and South Africa, to say nothing of Gibraltar.

Whether he liked it or not – and he probably didn't – Kopul Rosen would go to the countries that supplied his pupils on fundraising missions for his favourite cause, his school.

'But he always would be back for Friday nights and Shabbat.' After all, as Momy said, 'he was the soul of Carmel. We haven't got saints in Judaism, but we had Kopul Rosen.'

On those Friday nights, the eve of the Sabbath, Bella supervised the traditional Shabbat meal, lit the candles and sat next to her husband

and all the resident teachers. It was not an easy combination, but, Momy says, 'she did it all beautifully'. He continued:

> She was a very good-looking woman, an appearance which went well with her handsome husband. Very sweet. She knew how to talk to students. Sometimes, when they had problems, she would help out – a very good psychologist or therapist. They would be there with their sons and their little daughter.

He remembered the *zemirot*, the songs sung at the Sabbath table, obviously never to be forgotten: 'Now, when we have guests of our own in Gibraltar, I sing all the songs, although I have forgotten so much more. People say, "How do you know these songs so well?" I always reply in two words, "Carmel College".' There are so many reasons, as by now will be obvious, to use those words in answer to some religious or cultural question, but nothing can alter the fact that Carmel College is the inspiration behind so much that he does.

We talked about all this, Momy and I, but, again and again, we returned to the food. It seems he was so overwhelmed with the stew and other delights, he missed out the most important part of the eve of Shabbat meal – which confounded the belief that they only served English food at Carmel: 'Of course, there was the soup – chicken soup, naturally.' Naturally. 'Then we would sing the *zemirot*. Then there was chicken – and that famous dessert.'

Clearly, this was the pièce de résistance of the week. Momy says that, with the taste of the dessert still in his mouth, it was a good setting-off point for the half-an-hour's chat they were allowed between Shabbat eve dinner and bedtime. It was an old-fashioned world, and children's bedtime was strictly observed, as though it were part of the religious ritual. They must go to bed by 9.30 (which in those days was considered late for young boys and was a Shabbat treat) or accept the consequences. What those consequences were was never really spelt out, except to those who decided to use that extra half-hour to escape into the gardens for a smoke, which was strictly forbidden on the Sabbath in Jewish law, and not just for boys from Carmel College, who weren't allowed to light up at any other time, either.

But it has to be admitted that, on the whole, the Carmel boys did as they were told in the early 1950s – even the non-religious ones, and there were always a number of those, boys who had to adhere to the same rituals and rules as those for whom the prayers and the singing of table hymns was as natural as having their three meals a day. Those who didn't had the wrath of God and his representative on the earth of Oxfordshire, Kopul Rosen, come down on them. The 'good' boys – the ones who didn't break any of the rules – were allowed out into the town of Wallingford on Tuesday afternoons, as compensation for full discipline on Saturdays: 'We used to go there and into a café for a cup of tea. Some of the boys would eat a meal out, but, of course, I never did that. They weren't all as religiously brought up as I had been and had had enough of kashrut when they were in school.'

Kopul Rosen never despaired over the boys who were not particularly religious. As Momy recalled: 'He used to say, "I'm quite happy, even if I make one alone religious, I shall be satisfied." To this day, I meet some of them and they still keep, well, tradition, rather than religion. And, of course, there were, after a time, non-Jewish boys admitted and girls, too, later on.'

They had to be up at 8 o'clock on Saturday mornings, with coffee and cakes served at 9 o'clock, and then went to synagogue in the big hall, and there was always a 'very nice' Sabbath lunch. The 'bad' boys of Friday night were kept in on Tuesdays for detentions that could go on for weeks. Nobody was allowed out of the campus at weekends.

Perhaps all this was merely a reflection of the world of the 1950s, a decade of hope (or *tikva*, as the boys at Carmel were no doubt taught in their Hebrew lessons), but also of self-discipline in a community seemingly untouched by the world around it. Gangs who called themselves mods and rockers revolted and went on scooter rides to places such as Brighton which were always good for a punch-up scene. Cinema seats were torn up with the arrival on screen of Bill Hayley and the Comets, probably the first rock 'n' roll band, certainly to come to Britain. The world was changing. To the boys at Carmel College – and to their parents – it wasn't. That was clearly Carmel's strength, and it would possibly, in the fairly distant future, half a century after its foundation, prove to be its weakness. Momy has no memory of anything but strengths and, it seems, had no objections to the discipline at his old alma mater. He even has only good thoughts about Shabbat discipline at Carmel. Of course, he was brought up to – using the biblical term – honour the Sabbath day and make it holy. But the man who would join the army and then take up high office in his homeland was made to respect authority. When it came to Shabbat at Carmel College, he was in his seventh heaven (or even eighth or ninth, should that have existed).

In that spirit, he says of those weekly moments: 'It was out of this world. We had the top table, all the teachers coming along – including the non-Jewish ones, and they were in the majority. We would all be sitting there. Then Rabbi Rosen came in and we stood up, the whole school. Everybody had their best suits on.'

That was another feature of the education that Momy received, care of Carmel – a school that was not cheap. When the school closed, the fees amounted to some £30,000 a year. As we have already seen, it was a lot less expensive when Momy and his brother were there, but it still called for sacrifices:

> It was very hard for my father, who liked to be able to have new suits every year. When we were at Carmel, he couldn't do so. He was always well dressed – if not quite as well dressed as I like to

> be. My mother thought he could do better. She used to call, 'Isaac' and he'd answer 'All right. I'm clean.'

But Momy decided to do what he could. He sold his first collection of toy soldiers to help pay his way: 'I said to myself, "I'm going to sell them all and the money will be my pocket money when I'm in school and my father won't have to give me any more money."' We were not talking about lead soldiers from Woolworths, the sort that babies grabbed hold of, sucked and then went down with lead poisoning. He says they were worth a great deal more, a total of about £4,500. 'I had taken them with me to school, but I then said to myself, "Please God when I start work I'll, as they say in the army, replenish ammunition." And I did, I started to buy them again.' Now his collection has pride of place in the centre of his office in a glass case – the soul of an office cluttered with amazing artefacts. In fact, I suggested to him that it ought to become the Gibraltar Museum.

Now, that should not give the impression of Momy Levy, the good boy, actually being a 'goody goody' boy. As Robert Seruya remembered for me: 'I think we were both average academic students, but displayed a strong inclination for the girls and the nursing staff – to the extent that we would sometimes find ourselves being very well when unwell.'

There would be a few problems in Momy's last year. In his son Isaac's time at Carmel, girls were admitted as pupils to Carmel. In Momy's day, when there was not that additional attraction, the boys had to look outside the student body. As he says, he can confirm everything Robert Seruya says about the charms of the nursing staff. 'I got very friendly with the matron at Carmel', he recalled. 'Matron' gives the impression of a big busty woman with a loud voice that put the fear of God into the patients of one of the least salubrious National Health hospitals. The one at Carmel was not like that – and when Momy offered to take her to the pictures, she was only too pleased to accept the invitation to see whatever was playing at the cinema in Oxford, or at what was then known as a 'picture palace'. Momy made the date for the time he finished his Spanish lesson in the city.

But there was one moment of crisis: 'A teacher saw me.' He was probably just jealous – and jealous enough to tell Rabbi Rosen all about it: 'I'll never forget that meeting with him. Although there were just a few words, I remember him uttering, "Momy! I never expected this."' Momy tried a feeble explanation. The principal wasn't having it. 'Go, go away, boy!' Momy mumbled 'I am sorry, sir' and left.

As Robert Seruya says: 'We were bird watchers together. We always managed to find one for me and one for him.' That was, of course, one of the secrets to which the older members of Gibraltar Jewry were not kept apprised. Seruya put it like this: 'We were much more proficient in that part of our studies than on the academic side. But we were young men – and the hormones started to function and there was nothing else around in what was strictly a boys' school. As for the official studies, we were very, very average students – both of us.' But in the study of friendship, they were far from average: 'We were very close and have remained so through the years. Being at Carmel fostered that tremendously.'

Holidays presented something of a problem. In the long summer break, Momy would go back home to Gibraltar. At Christmas (Chanukah) he either stayed behind at the school or with friends.

I couldn't help wondering whether the life in a boarding school like Carmel was somewhat artificial. Not so, says Momy: 'There was nothing artificial about it. Everything was normal – it was as if it had been an ordinary grammar school. It always seemed very natural. And the standard of education, I have always been led to understand, was very high.' He took time to reflect on this and on what would inevitably appear to be the crunch question. What did he miss by being away from home? 'It wasn't always easy, but I was made to feel as if I was really at home. And I did.'

In July 1955, he said goodbye to that 'home'. Four friends left at the same time. 'We shook hands, said we would keep in touch. We did.' But not, to Momy's everlasting dismay, with Kopul Rosen: 'I did intend to keep up our relationship, but I went to London to work and then to Gibraltar and sadly he passed away.' As we have seen, Kopul Rosen died of leukaemia in 1962 at the age of 48.

All in all, Carmel's place in Momy's life was an injection of a substance that he is sure still flows through his veins:

> I can say, and it's an expression you've heard a thousand times but is wholly true in this case, the school made me a man.
>
> For one thing, it taught me values – the value of the dignity of life. It also taught me the value of money. I got to know what a pound is and what a penny is – you know that other cliché, look after the pennies and the pounds will look after themselves. The school emphasized that for me.
>
> There had been a time, even at the wonderful Carmel College, when I was severely broke. The food was good, but I was really hungry sometimes. I'd take a slice of bread, put gravy on it and have three or four pieces of bread. But the food, I have to admit, was reasonable. Small boys have big appetites and the value of what was needed to stem that need for extra food was one of the things I learned.
>
> I know we were lucky in all that we had at home – in Gibraltar, my family had a little Citroën. My friends' fathers drove Jaguars. I never worried about that. Thank God, all my life I have accepted it and enjoyed what I have.

And always he will say that having the memories of Carmel College and its charismatic principal are high on that list of what he has.

He left with all colours flying. In his final report, Kopul Rosen wrote what in a working life would be called a reference:

> Solomon Levy has been a pupil at Carmel College since September 1950 and I've had ample opportunity of observing him closely. He's a sincere and industrious student, very hard working, although not spectacular. As a prefect he has discharged his duties with a sense of fairness and is deservedly popular and respected. His health is good and, although not highly skilled in sports, [he] has nevertheless endeavoured to take an active part in them. I also have the advantage of knowing his family background in Gibraltar. The Levy family is noted for its industry and integrity. The boy's uncle is the Mayor of Gibraltar. I consider Solomon Levy eminently suitable for admission to an English university and I would recommend him without reservations.

Sir Peter Russo, the solicitor with whom Isaac Levy worked for years, also provided a reference. Isaac had been invited to continue to use Sir Peter's office even after he retired. Now, he wrote about his notary public's son:

> I know Mr Solomon Levy of 5, Governors Lane, Gibraltar. He belongs to a respectable family of this colony. His character and conduct are exemplary and he's been a pupil at Carmel College, an English public school, for a few years until recently. He is seeking admission into an English university in October 1956 after completing his military service in this colony. I have pleasure in recommending him.

Momy decided not to go to university. As he had realized a long time ago, and as Rabbi Rosen wrote, his academic achievements were not 'spectacular'. Besides, when he left Carmel, he couldn't wait to go home and wasn't changing his mind now.

But to this day he remains devoted to his memories of school at Newbury and Wallingford and his charismatic head teacher. 'I can tell you, Momy Levy would not have been Momy Levy without Carmel College', he says. 'Even my life in Gibraltar has been dictated by what I learned at Carmel College – and not just [from] Kopul Rosen. Also, I shall always thank my parents for having sent me there.'

IN THE ARMY NOW

I know I am known now as the most monarchist person in Gibraltar. I don't mind that, just so long as they don't call me a bastard!

Solomon Levy

It was an old Jewish joke come alive. Momy was a soldier and his mother Rachel was worried that he was not going to get enough food. So she cooked him his usual meals and took them down to his barracks. Forget the old American injunction, 'send a salami to your boy in the army', Mrs Levy sent herself – with a basket of the best Sephardi food her son could imagine.

It happened after he left school in 1955. He started at the barracks of the Gibraltar Defence Force – eventually to become the Royal Gibraltar Regiment – because he was 18 years old and had six months' National Service to do – which was eighteen months less than he would have had to offer on behalf of his Queen and country had he lived in Britain itself. But, as we have seen, the Gibraltar Government believed it had to do its bit, and putting Solomon Levy in uniform was part of its contribution.

On the now four-hour flight (the planes had been changed so there were no stops for refuelling) from London to the Rock, the first as no longer a schoolboy, Momy had a lot to contemplate. One was, of course, the fact that he was no longer at Carmel College, which in itself meant a huge change in his life pattern. Another was settling in at home, to which he was very much looking forward. He was still very much a young family man and the thought of being back in the heart of that family was wonderful – kissing and hugging his mother and father ... and, not least, having his mother's cooking every day. Except, of course, he knew that he wouldn't get it every day unless some arrangement could be made.

There was also going to be a certain need if he was going to get on – to learn to drive. His father came to his aid, as he usually (but, as we shall see, only 'usually') did:

> My dad had made some money by then and he bought himself that Citroën car and I learnt to drive in it. It was one of those big, grey, old-style cars you can now see in the movies. It was two in the front and three in the back. My father took us out every Sunday with our chauffeur driving our car.

There was no reason for his love of Britain vis-à-vis Spain to stop him enjoying the Iberian peninsula.

Before the family contemplated the possibility of any of those arrangements for feeding their eldest child, there was another thing to be gone into: Momy's future career. His army service was about to happen, but it was for just six months and he was unlikely to be sent abroad, so, in addition to discussing menus with his mother, there was the important matter of what was going to happen when he finally got out of uniform.

Momy decided he wanted to be a lawyer. Isaac Levy decided he didn't think it was a good idea and since his father's word remained law, as decisive as anything Kopul Rosen had laid down, Momy had to think again. Nobody now knows what sort of a lawyer he would have made. With the benefit of hindsight of the twenty-twenty variety, there's a lot to suggest that he might have done very well. He is and was then a man of compassion and understanding – qualities not to be overlooked. But his father thought otherwise. He said, 'Momy, if you go into that court, before you start the case, the judge would know exactly what you're going to tell him. You can't do it ... you can't. Forget it. Please.'

It was hard saying yes to Isaac, but just as a previous man with that name had to wrestle with being about to be sacrificed, he decided that this one wasn't going to lose out. He ordered his son to think again. 'Look, Momy', he added, 'I've worked with lawyers for forty years. I know what the law's all about and you won't make it.'

Momy says there was no ill feeling when their father raised no objection to his youngest son James going into the law – and becoming brilliantly successful, at that. They were very different: 'My father was right. I am glad he said that. James can argue. I can't.' But in time he did become a magistrate, and allowed others to do the arguing in front of him.

After their somewhat disheartening discussion, Momy sent off a letter to the Temple in London for which he had first applied to say that he no longer intended following the profession. Besides, there was the question of wearing that uniform to consider.

He was already a year behind the other National Servicemen in the Defence Corps – if you asked any of them what they were defending, they might well have said their homeland against Spain – and was anxious to do his bit, providing it didn't interfere with Sunday afternoon drives to Malaga. 'I was only a private, but perhaps because it was such a small outfit, I was allowed many privileges – to keep Shabbat and the festivals, for one thing.' On the other hand, he made his contribution towards returning the compliments: 'One Christmas I was the only one in the entire barracks. Everyone else was given leave and I was there to hold the fort, literally.'

Presumably the news was passed on to General Franco, who knew that with Private Solomon Levy in charge of his nation's defences he really did have to think twice about the idea of taking the Rock by force – and how could you blame him? Momy Levy was in uniform, with doubtless the smartest, best-pressed tunic and trousers in the entire barracks.

He was stationed alongside a division of the Seaforth Highlanders. I asked Momy if he had to wear a kilt. 'Me? No.' And not because Jewish law would frown on such things. Momy is a man without prejudices. Certainly he has nothing against the Scots. But there were distinct problems with the men from the bonny Highlands who were there with him. Particularly the drill instructors – who did wear the tartan kilt:

> If I had been in the army for five years, not just six months, I would still not have understood what they were saying to – or rather shouting at – me. Their accents totally beat me. Not that I was the only one. Several of the recruits were living in Spain, in the border town of La Linea – and they were totally defeated.

Maybe that would have been the answer had the Spanish invaded after all – they couldn't possibly win any battle of words with the Highlanders. 'Those men were actually very good instructors. There were about fifty of them.'

The hardest time for Momy was, as with every other recruit, the first ten days: 'It was basic training and in those ten days they attempted to make us soldiers.' In the British army that was called 'square bashing'. The square being the one outside the barracks, where sergeants would bark orders and insults in equal measure, questioning the parentage of every young man under their control (and control it certainly was) and stating in no uncertain terms that Momy and everyone else owing allegiance to the then young and beautiful Queen were the lowest form of animal life. Even coupling them with animals was something of a compliment.

Momy recalls: 'We got our uniform and learned how to salute. You were told how you had to act as a soldier.' Discipline was particularly tough and nothing like the reasonable rules emanating from Dr Kopul Rosen's study. It wasn't exactly a life full of financial riches to match the ones that military life seemed to offer in the form of lovely warm feelings of doing good work. 'I was paid the pre-decimal equivalent of £1.26 a week. And I didn't touch a penny of it. My parents were helping me. Mind you, several of my fellow soldiers had to use it. Afterwards, I added up those wages and spent it all – on a white dinner jacket. I adored that.' Which wouldn't have surprised anyone who knew him, even then.

He did something in the army which wasn't on the agenda for the other recruits: 'My uncle, Sir Joshua, told me, "Right. You put on your uniform and go to the Jewish transit camp [the one in which those immigrants from Morocco were housed before they were flown to Israel] and start washing plates there."' That was one thing about being scion of a family such as the Levys. Momy would never deny that he has been privileged, but, as the royal family are wont to say, with privilege comes responsibility. Washing plates (and saucepans) seemed to sum that up. It wasn't exactly a job young soldiers would queue up to do.

Whether he planned to spend his military earnings on a jacket while he was serving he cannot now remember. But the routine in the Buena Vista barracks, facing Europa Point with its famous lighthouse, is engraved on his memory: 'They would let me off early on Fridays and, in return, I did the required duty on Sundays.'

In between, his mother met his dietary needs. He wasn't the only one with special self-created facilities for food:

> Several of the boys used to have a rope fixed to a basket, which their mums would come and fill with food, which was then hauled over the high wall outside the barracks, and their fam-

> ilies would come and bring them cigarettes and chocolates. My mother did it less dramatically. She would come to the guardroom and leave a basket filled with kosher goodies for me to pick up. My dear mother, bless her, did it twice a day. She would drive to the guardroom in her own car and give me lunch and then supper. I was lucky; compared with what I heard about real army food, you could say I was extremely privileged.

Yes, you could say that. Momy would go down to the guardroom and pick up the basket (sometimes the food was wrapped in a towel), consume the contents and, feeling suitably satisfied, bring the empty container back to the guardroom. His mother would collect the empties while bringing the fresh supplies.

He admitted he was teased by the other youngsters, but none of it was cruel: 'After having been in a boys' school for five years, army life wasn't as difficult for me as it was for some of the other recruits – who had never left their houses for more than five minutes at a time, or so it seemed.'

The army became one of those drugs that keep Momy on a continuous high, a combination of just loving to be with people and a genuine feeling that he is doing some good. Besides which, he thought that if he were a total civilian he would miss the uniform – although he thought he could do better if he were an officer. So he became a second lieutenant. The way he tells it, this was the most obvious and simple thing he could do:

> I had done my National Service, all six months of it. But four years later, in April 1960, I became concerned that the Gibraltar Defence Force, as it then was, had no Jewish officers. [Later, a former Gibraltar governor, Richard Luce who was to become Lord Chamberlain arranged for its name to be changed to the

> Royal Gibraltar Regiment.] That to me was a situation that had to be changed. And then a few weeks later, I saw that the Force were advertising three vacant commissions. Well, I couldn't resist that. I went in front of a selection board – all colonels. And they asked me: 'What's your connection with the army?' I said, 'None.' So they came back: 'Why are you here then?' I said 'Because there are no Jews in the regiment. I think it would be good for both of us – and I want to mix.'

It would merit high in any chutzpah index, but Private Momy Levy (Retired) felt he had nothing to lose. They either said 'Yes' and he rested on his unsullied but not particularly glorious National Service laurels or they said 'No' and it would be goodbye to all this. But that chutzpah index almost left the scale. He decided that telling them he would be good for the regiment was one thing, but he was the one who had to state conditions to his application: 'I told them, "If you pick me to be an officer, I have to insist on one or two things. I cannot come on Saturdays and I will not come on the festivals – unless there was an emergency and, of course, I would come."'

One can imagine what would have happened in Britain. The colonels would have twiddled their moustaches, spluttered into their whisky glasses and made, under their breath, a few remarks that would not be considered particularly pleasant about people of Mr Solomon Levy's religion. But this was Gibraltar. This was a military force that needed people with go and initiative. And this was a regiment that was not overwhelmed with applications. Three weeks later, Momy received a letter with an impressive crest on the notepaper. Mr Levy could be enrolled as a second lieutenant in the reserve. Welcome.

His army experience also helped cement interfaith relations:

> On one occasion, they made the local priest Bishop of Gibraltar and there were big celebrations here on the Rock. I heard them

> say that they needed a regimental contribution to that commemoration. The call went up: 'We need one officer and twenty men in Main Street, so that when he goes to the church, there's a group of soldiers to present arms.' As soon as I heard that, I went to the colonel and said, 'I want to be that officer.'

All well and good. Momy was plainly a competent enough officer – except there was one real problem. He had an antipathy to handling a sword. Now, how he became an officer while saying 'I don't intend to pick up a sword' and no one complained of yet another *chutzpahdik* black mark is another story. 'I said I can't go on parade for that reason' – and nobody objected. But now he was volunteering to lead a parade and the colonel was, understandably, somewhat bewildered, to say the least: 'YOU want to be the officer? But didn't you tell me you didn't want to be on parades?'

> I said, 'Yes, but this is special.' And for two months I would go to the barracks at 8 o'clock in the morning to practise my sword drill. And when the time came, the bishop processed to the church and I was the one there to shout, 'Present ...', you know, shouting it properly and screaming the second word, 'arms!'

Now, as a reserve officer, his mother wasn't expected to deliver his meals in her baskets. 'I had to eat in the mess for meals. They usually had boiled eggs, smoked salmon and other fish. So I always had something to eat.'

He would like to have become a captain – once he had ceased to be a full lieutenant, that is. On the other hand, every time there was a promotion course, it turned out to be on a religious festival. So he had to be content with first one and then two pips (officially called 'stars') on his shoulder. The third, which made him a captain, would take somewhat longer – about a year.

But the chutzpah went on – and to the benefit of the regiment. That was when he gave them his Christmas present. 'I told the commanding officer, "Look, colonel. I'm coming here on Christmas Day early in the morning. I am relieving the whole guard and I'm taking command of the whole Buena Vista Barracks."' It sounded like an ultimatum from a conquering army, talking to a defeated officer carrying a white flag. But there was no white flag. The colonel got up from his chair, thanked his new captain vociferously, slapped him on the back and was ready to tell his men that Christmas was saved. Santa Claus was named Momy Levy. That actually was about it:

> The local newspaper gave it headlines – a photograph of me on my own in the barracks. As they wrote, 'Momy takes over guard on Christmas so that his friends can go home.' And it wasn't just the colonel who was impressed. There was a brigadier who seemed quite happy, too.
>
> There were other regiments here in Gibraltar and he used to go round and visit them all. When he came to our barracks – actually *my* barracks, that day – he was very nice. He knew I couldn't eat the mince pies and other goodies. So he came with a beer, which he knew I could have, and we'd sit there and have a chat. The other men came back at midnight – and I went home.

He says it was a way of reversing his military situation – a means of saying thank you.

But, nevertheless, as we have seen, he really did do that duty, in strange ways that involved a rabbinical dispensation and the avoidance of what could easily have been a military catastrophe. For, among all the days in uniform, one stands out even when placed head to head with learning how to use a sword so that he could lead the parade at the bishop's consecration. One could say that was yet another example of the interfaith relations that exist in Gibraltar.

This was another event in Momy's military career that could merit a place in the regimental history books. It was also a tribute to the constant devotion of Momy to the Queen. It was Her Majesty's official birthday. Traditionally, the day is celebrated on a Saturday – by Trooping the Colour on Horse Guards Parade in London and by the firing of guns of salute by the Royal Gibraltar Regiment on the Rock (insignificant other salutes are fired in little places such as Canada, Australia and New Zealand, but Gibraltar's is vital). On this particular Royal Salute day, Momy was asked, as an artillery specialist, to man the gun party. 'Erm ... I'm not sure that I can ... ahm ... a great honour, but ... may I think it over?' He was told by his friend the colonel that he could certainly think it over – although the colonel possibly added under his breath, 'providing he says yes'.

Actually, it wasn't so much Momy himself thinking it over as his rabbi, who was immediately called in on this ticklish diplomatic and military problem. 'I told him that, of course, I would walk to the rock, where the firing by the guns would take place. A long walk, but I could do it.' But the principal point of the exercise was firing the guns. That surely was not part of the ritual of the holy Sabbath. And even if, in some quarters, it was, surely actually firing a gun on Shabbat had to be forbidden in a religion that didn't even allow the turning on of an electric light switch and which offered the greeting 'Shabbat Shalom'.

The rabbi thought about it, no doubt consulting the appropriate Talmudic tract, and began asking questions – which, in Judaism, is always a difficult thing to do, since, traditionally, asking a question leads to another question. But the rabbi stroked his beard and asked just the same: 'What would your job be?' 'Leading the gun party', Momy replied. Another movement by the rabbi to his beard. This time, a slight tug. 'And you fire the guns?' 'No', said the ever-anxious Captain Levy. 'You don't fire the gun?' 'No', replied Momy. 'So who does fire the guns?' 'The soldiers', he replied. 'So what do you do?' 'I give the orders. I have to shout "Fire!" That's all.' 'That's all?' 'That's all', Momy emphasized. The rabbi looked at him, staring directly into his eyes. 'So go ahead', said the rabbi, 'Shout as long as you like. Shabbat shalom.' A Sabbath of peace – except, of course, while Momy is shouting 'Fire' the cannons open up with a not too Shabbat shalom-like sound. The Governor, Sir Adrian Johns, told me: 'I love that story, but Momy admits that he was always worried about what would happen if the Spanish invaded on a Saturday.' One imagines that the rabbi would have been equally indulgent. You can do all sorts of things to save life in the Jewish religion. Including fighting a war in Israel on Yom Kippur, the holiest day of all.

Whatever the might-have-beens, this alone was the prelude to a record in the Royal Salute business. He was to chalk up no fewer than 175 occasions when he gave that instruction to 'Fire'. The Queen's birthday always became his job. Then when a visiting Royal Navy ship sailed in, he had to supervise the fifteen-gun salute. An admiral would get anything from seven guns to twenty-one, all fired on four twenty-five-pounder guns.

Momy held the record not only for the number of salutes, to which he took like a rabbi to his prayer book, but also for being the lowest-ranking officer to be in charge of the gun battery – which he says he was with every day of his reserve service: 'The other officers who did this were all majors. Now, I should have become a major, too. But because of all the Jewish holidays I took off, I still kept missing courses.'

Momy served in the regiment for eighteen years, until 1978. On his forty-second birthday, he was 'dined out' at the barracks by his fellow officers as a gesture of friendly farewell:

> There was a shop in Gibraltar that sold American-made 'Empire' kosher chicken. The colonel knew that I liked having meat, especially on an occasion like this. He knew that he couldn't cook it for me, so he bought sixty Empire chickens so that everyone there had the same kosher food. My friends told me it didn't taste any different from non-kosher chickens.

He may have left the army, but his association with it continued for years afterwards. He was a member of the Gibraltar Regiment Association. Looking back now, he says it was just one more example of the population of Gibraltar feeling as if it were one big family – and, the way he tells it, a happy family at that.

Only those who have never met Momy Levy would be surprised at the success of the relationship between him and Her Majesty's Royal Gibraltar Regiment. To those who either know him well or have merely been in his company, it would be no surprise at all. And yet it is worth stopping for a moment to analyse the situation. An Orthodox Jew – despite his protestations, and, compared with most people who give themselves that appellation, a *really* Orthodox Jew who has not stopped 'laying *tefillin*', putting on the phylacteries that go with morning prayers, for a single day, apart from when he was recovering from the serious operation we shall discuss later on; it is an unusual combination. But it all goes together with the bowler hat and the walking stick and the rest of what appears, to the promenaders down Main Street, to be his regalia. He loves ceremony and all that goes with it. He also loves Gibraltar, and if an outfit like the Royal Gibraltar Regiment was there to protect his beloved country, it is hardly surprising he wanted a part in it.

It is also safe to say that this was appreciated on both sides of the fence, or what in other places would be considered the religious divide. Except, as we have already witnessed, there is little or no divide between the religions and the cultures in this amazing little nation. If there were, it is not beyond the imagination to think of Momy getting hold of one of those guns his soldiers fired and putting matters to right. That is, of course, after knocking the heads together in person of the people who caused the dispute. He wouldn't hesitate to do that. He would probably put another banner outside his office or have some postage stamps printed, all declaring the word 'unity'.

One can't help speculating further. What if Gibraltar were not still connected, even if just loosely, with Britain? Not as part of Spain, but as an independent nation, which the population have constantly rejected. Would Momy not qualify as Gibraltar's ambassador to the United Kingdom, the United States, Israel? No one else would come close. But with his National Service army career at an end and no need for his mother to come twice a day with her basket of kosher food, Solomon Levy, Private (Retired), had to take his life to another stage.

THE WORKING MAN

Estate agents have the reputation for being sharks. I can assure you I'm no shark.

Solomon Levy

Going out to work for the first time can be a traumatic experience. For Momy it was more than an experience, it was a life changer.

This was yet another example of how different things were in the 1950s. Young people left school or, in the case of a fortunate few, university with one certainty – they would all find jobs. It was an age of full employment and the only question to ask was 'what should I do?' Very, very few anticipated being out of work. The Labour Government in Britain had promised that there would be no recurrence of the workless lines that followed the end of the First World War, and it was a promise kept.

Of course, what happened in Britain was reflected in its then colony of Gibraltar. There was an age of austerity, and if it was not felt so deeply on the Rock, its repercussions were. Foodstuffs that had been brought in regularly from England in pre-Second World War days were extraordinarily limited. But things had changed remarkably. The Festival of Britain in 1951 established a mood of optimism and that, too, was echoed in Gibraltar's life. The accession of Queen Elizabeth II the following year ushered in what was claimed to be a new Elizabethan Age. At Carmel College, the young royalist named Levy rejoiced (and hasn't stopped rejoicing since).

When Momy left the army – the full-time army, that is – he had an air of a maturity that was not nearly so obvious in the school leavers looking for and finding work. There was, however, a problem for him and for every other youngster about to join what was called the 'labour market'; going into a profession that would carry him through his whole working life couldn't be done, adequately at least, in Gibraltar. The nearest country to the Rock was Spain, a fifteen-minute walk away from Governor's Lane. But any qualifications he could get in Spain in normal times wouldn't have carried much weight in what was now an Anglo-Saxon world, where speaking English correctly was a necessary passport to success. And even if Momy had followed that path, he would have recognized that these were not normal times. General Franco would not have been exactly a help. There was only one place for Momy: he would have to go back to England.

Had he got his way, he would have had to go to London to study law. And every other career of worth would have required exactly the same step. His father sealed his fate in that regard. Having told his eldest son that he was certain he would not make a barrister or even a solicitor, he put the ball back in Momy's court, allowing him at least the semblance of choosing his own future: 'Why don't you think of something else?' It was a loaded question. Of course he had to think of something else. 'So I said to him, "Would you mind if I became an estate agent?"' This was another example of how different the world of the 1950s was from that of sixty years later. It is almost incredible to imagine a son asking permission in that way, but young people who considered themselves well brought up were doing it all over the world. It was almost like a young man asking his prospective bride's father for permission to marry his daughter.

This time the senior Mr Levy was more indulgent: 'He said to me, "I'm a part-time estate agent, so you do that".' It was a cause for celebration. But it would mean leaving home, and one of the great things about saying goodbye to Carmel College had been breathing in the fresh sea air of Gibraltar. Momy started making his plans, signed up with a Jewish property company in London and booked his ticket for another four-hour flight to what was becoming known as London Airport. The new job was assured and so was a new place of learning. But no Kopul Rosen awaited him, ready to greet him with a hand on his shoulder.

His boss at the Westcliff and London Property company was a well-known Anglo-Jewish figure named Harry Landy, who was not in the least a Kopul Rosen figure. But the job was quite an education: 'For the first month, I was in the repairs department, going out with inspectors, and then I went out seeing properties and making a report back at the office. They owned properties all over.'

The advantage of looking at broken drains and ceilings that had found a way of falling into living rooms was the travel from one end of London to the other. 'I got to know London pretty well', he agreed. 'What was very special for me was "The Good Loo Guide". You had to know that sort of thing when you went travelling in 1960. I once asked my father if he had ever seen a toilet with green tiles. He answered: "I didn't send you to London to inspect toilets."'

Despite his years at Carmel College, Momy knew his English needed brushing up: 'I would always say, for instance, "Thanks, God." And there was an English lady in the company who helped me. I'll never forget her name. It was Miss Hackett. She sort of took me under her wing.' Whether she was responsible for changing his name, temporarily, that is, is another matter: 'I thought that calling myself Solomon was not all that good in London and I really couldn't be Momy there either. In England, it sounded like "Mummy" and a Mummy I certainly wasn't and was unlikely to become one after I died either.' That was how he got to be called Stephen: 'So I was called

Stephen and Miss Hackett always called me that. One day she heard me say "Thanks, God" and told me, "Stephen, say 'Thank God', not 'Thanks God'."' God undoubtedly understood. Isaac Levy wasn't so sure. Momy's father saw a letter signed 'Stephen Levy' and didn't altogether like it: 'Who the hell is Stephen Levy?' he asked. 'I've never heard of such a person.'

Not many people knew of anyone like Harry Landy, either. He was not the most approachable of men, unless those who did approach him were ready to pay their rent without giving any trouble. 'He never said, "Good morning" to me, never to anybody. But I was to become the most popular person in the office in 1957.' That was when Archie Lew, the manager in the repair department, was faced with the sort of question he had never had before. He was a small, tubby man, the brother of Dayan (a rabbi who had the status of a religious court judge) Myer Lew and another rabbi, so he was well versed in awkward questions. But not one of this kind.

'Can I have Thursday off?' Momy asked. 'Why?' Lew asked. 'To go to Buckingham Palace', he replied. 'Are you trying to be funny?' the manager asked. But Momy wasn't. The answer was a distinct 'No' – until, that is, Mr Lew had a telephone call.

'Hello', said the caller. 'My name is Joshua Hassan, I'm the Mayor of Gibraltar and I'm taking my nephew to Buckingham Palace. All right?' '"Oh yes", Archie replied, "Of course." The news resounded across the office. "Stephen's going to Buckingham Palace." I went to Moss Bros. Hired the outfit.'

If Mr Lew was taken aback, so was a certain bus conductor who also thought Momy was pulling his leg. He might have had strangely dressed people on his bus before. But people going to Buckingham Palace, particularly if they are kitted out by Moss Bros, usually go by car. Nobody would think of getting on a bus and going to a society wedding – or certainly not in the 1950s. But the conductor of the number 16 bus was a kind cockney who enjoyed the experience. 'Are you getting married, mate?' he asked.

'No', said Momy as he asked for a ticket to the Palace, sitting on the top deck in a morning suit and top hat. He might or might not have explained that it was the only way he could get to the palace for the Queen's investiture of his uncle as a Companion of the Order of the British Empire, CBE. Since Momy was the only relative of his in London at the time apart from his wife, the normally unemotional uncle was delighted to have him along. But he didn't dream of providing the transport – or even the dress suit.

'I got there very early and found a seat in the front row with my aunt, Joshua's wife', Momy said. 'I must say I felt proud – for my uncle, for our family, for the Jewish community and, most of all, I suppose, for Gibraltar.'

Back on the job, there were the odd human moments: 'I went into a property and the lady there could hardly speak. And I just said to her something in Spanish. She embraced me. She was an old lady from Gibraltar who had been evacuated to London and stayed. But she didn't have a word of English, even all those years after the war. She was literally afraid to speak to anyone.'

One other thing concerned him. He was as anxious about coming into contact with strange dogs as any postman:

> Before I'd go into a house I'd ask if they had a dog. If they did, I wouldn't go in. But there were two old ladies [Momy frequently found himself in contact with old ladies] whom I asked if they had a dog and one of them replied, 'Yeh. Only a small one. It's all right, all right.' So I go in – just in time for that bastard of a dog to attack me. He bit through my trousers – and my leg. There was a hospital nearby. I went there and they gave me a tetanus injection. I was told that after half an hour, I'd

> have a reaction. I asked what the reaction was. The doctor said, 'Don't worry son. You'll feel all right.' And he was right. But I was more worried about that reaction than anything.

The rest of his education was at evening classes at the College of Estate Management. At first, he wasn't what could be called the ideal student. A possible combination of overwork for Mr Landy & Co. and sheer boredom meant that, as likely as not, he would fall asleep – an effect usually reserved for listening to rabbis' sermons in synagogue. His father got to hear about it and treated the news with the same unhappy contempt he felt when he realized that Solomon Levy was no longer Solomon Levy, but a stranger called Stephen.

'I'm not sending you to London to fall asleep', he declared – and so Momy, always the dutiful son, did his best to stay awake. 'But it wasn't easy', he remembers.

Momy stayed with the company for two years and then spent another two, full time, at the college in Kensington. It was more stimulating than working for Mr Lew or Mr Landy. Although he did some work in the legal department (it was a very big concern in those days), occupying himself with leases and conveyancing, his time was spent mostly on repairs, which was not exactly the kind of work a nice Jewish boy from Gibraltar had dreamed of doing. But it was useful experience: 'I went out with inspectors and saw what they used to do and after six months I did it on my own.'

The college gave him his qualifications. He became a Fellow of the Society of Valuers and Auctioneers, which made him able to work as both a surveyor and an auctioneer. Meanwhile, the family who were his landlords moved from Maida Vale to Ladbroke Grove, further west in London, and Momy would go to work by the number 52 bus to Kensington High Street and then walk to his office behind the famous Barkers department store. He not only qualified, but made friendships, too – one of which is still part of his life to this day.

He also came into contact with Sir Cyril Black, the MP for Wimbledon, and no doubt used the Momy Levy magic in making friends and influencing people. Sir Cyril would prove to be a useful contact.

London was a bittersweet kind of experience. He was learning his profession and enjoying the fact that, despite all, he was making progress. He went to a Spanish club and met Spanish-speaking girls. But, on the whole, he admits he was 'very lonely'. For five years, he lodged with two sisters by the name of Benoliel, Sephardim from Gibraltar: 'They were very nice and treated me like a son. But I didn't get many invitations because I didn't know many people.' That turned out to be the spur to make sure in later years that he would always invite people for Shabbat lunch and dinner.

The Spanish club in the basement of a block of flats in Hall Road, called Grove Court, was by way of a breath of fresh air for him, away from the kindness of the two sisters. He needed to be able to mix with contemporaries: 'I used to go there every Saturday night from nine till about two and was one of about six Spanish-speaking chaps. It wasn't Jewish, but it gave me life for the next week.' Many a student in a strange town could relate to that, and to his quest for feminine company: 'They were all Spanish girls there, au pairs working in London. I used to ask them where they worked and invariably they would say, "I work with funny people. They don't put their lights on or off on Saturdays. They put them on on Fridays." I told them, "Yes, it must be very odd."' The girls were referring to the Orthodox Jewish restriction on using electricity on the Sabbath.

The girls did help him cope with London. So did a friend called Abie Massias, still one of his closest friends, with whom he would go to Hyde Park on Sundays to listen to the soapbox orators on Speakers' Corner. But London wasn't home, and the city could be a very lonely place. As he told me with a depth of feeling he still recalls from that time: 'In Gibraltar you live. In London, you survive.'

But there were the inevitable diversions. There were always girls in his life: 'After Hyde Park, we'd go to the Cumberland Hotel, for a cup of tea or coffee – which was a very good way to pick up a nice Jewish girl – and afterwards go to a dance. I knew which girls were Jewish and I'd go up to them and say, "Hello. My name is Solomon Levy"' – which left them in no doubt where his religious loyalties lay. And then he'd add, 'I'm from Gibraltar.' One of these girls was a pen friend he had made through a column in the *Jewish Chronicle*. It was the nearest the paper had to a lonely hearts section in those days – a 'come be my pen friend' column:

> She was a very nice girl and I had written to say I was coming to London. She lived in Swiss Cottage and we became very friendly. She always made a point of, wherever we went, getting a message through to the hotel's switchboard – and would then hear the loudspeakers proclaiming 'Will Sarah Parker go to a telephone.' She just loved to hear her name called out in a public place. She was a hairdresser somewhere and I had to say to her, 'Look darling, no marriage. We're going out as friends.' Then her mother started pressing. So I said, 'Nice knowing you and bye bye.'

Nice man, Mr Solomon Levy – or certainly that was what she thought. 'She was a bit upset', he remembers, which might or might not be an understatement.

'I always behaved myself', he assured me, which possibly smoothed his path with girls, Jewish or otherwise. With the Spanish au pairs, his line was, 'I respect you. But you're not Jewish ...'. One caught him off guard. 'But I'm Jewish', she said. But I stuck to my word.'

He liked to appear dapper, even in those days, complete with bow tie: 'I was dancing with one girl and the bow tie fell off. She couldn't stop laughing. "What's the matter?" I asked her. "Well," she said, "if my daddy knew I was going out with a boy wearing a clip-on tie, I don't know what he'd say." To which I replied, "Well, darling, I'm going out with you, not your daddy."'

But these were just diversions. No doubt Mr and Mrs Levy of Governor's Lane would have appreciated the news that these ladies were not for turning – into wives, particularly if they had heard about the Spanish au pairs. Meanwhile, Momy couldn't wait to get home.

'Yes, I was very lonely', he repeated. 'I don't like big places. I'm a lazy so-and-so. I like to get up, walk five minutes and be at work. I like to walk down Main Street and see people I know.'

The opportunity to do just that came in April 1960. He had taken his final exams on 30 March 1960. He didn't bother to wait for the results – as we have seen, he passed – and got on the first plane back home.

The day after his arrival back in Gibraltar, on 1 April (which turned out to be more auspicious than many associate with the famed April Fools' Day), he opened his office with the name emblazoned on the windows, 'Solomon Levy, Estate Agents'.

His name on the office door was the first statement that Solomon Levy had arrived and was going public. The judgment of this Solomon that he could make a success of the job proved right. That seems to have convinced the population of Gibraltar well enough. He was one of only four agents on the Rock. His firm is still there.

He also went into the building society business, and called in an old friendship: 'There were no building societies in Gibraltar. But I remembered that Sir Cyril Black was chairman of building societies in Britain and also on the Temperance Building Society in Barbados.' He was interested in the idea of setting up one on the Rock. The only trouble was that such establishments not only did not exist in Gibraltar, they would not have been legal. So more influence was called on. Momy rang Sir Joshua, who immediately (to coin a cliché) put the wheels in motion:

> He introduced a new law to cater for building societies. So we opened the Gibraltar Building Society. Sir Cyril Black was chairman and another director was Sir Frederick Bennett, MP for Torbay, and he joined the board. I, too, became a director, with another man. My friends couldn't understand at first what we were doing. Several asked, 'So what are you going to build?'

Sir Cyril was a deeply religious man, a Methodist lay preacher: 'When he came to Gibraltar I used to go with him to the local Methodist Church and tell the minister that he was coming – and when he did, he used to preach at their Sunday service.'

Momy admits that he wasn't the best-behaved young Jewish man about town, either in London or Gibraltar. As this thoroughly upright leader of his synagogue remembers, he put in quite a bit of mileage in the furtherance of his quest for girlfriends. Unsurprisingly, his parents got to hear about it and were seriously worried. 'Very worried indeed', Momy added. 'They thought I was going to fall into the trap. I mean, I was nine years a bachelor.'

Actually, a lot of people got to hear about Momy's activities with young ladies – and about his sports car. The red MG which he had used for serenading (well, there's no actual record of his singing) was featured in *Vogue* magazine. It is possible that they saw Momy's choice of dress and decided that here was a man who would match the women glorifying their pages. The problem was that it was his car the magazine wanted, not himself.

He was too canny a cookie to let them get away with it just like that. 'The magazine', he explained to me, 'came to Gibraltar to promote the MG and a set of suitcases. My car was the one they wanted and [they] asked me to lend my car to them for ten days. I said, "No. I will come with the car, or no car – wherever you want it, [tell me] and I'll be with you." We stayed for ten days in the Don Pepe Hotel in Marbella.'

The car wasn't featured on its own – or, to Momy's extreme regret, with him in the pictures. They had four models to show off dresses as well as a car: 'They took me around with them – to Ronda on one day, which I enjoyed very much; they have a great bullring and, as you know, I love bullfights.'

But there were no fights of any kind on the trip, which he enjoyed thoroughly: all expenses paid, hotel, food, everything. But they didn't pay him, which I suggested was a surprising neglect on Momy's part. He did enjoy being with the models, as he did with numerous other ladies whom he and his MG took to Marbella frequently enough for his parents to worry more. 'Oh yes, they were very worried, extra worried. But I used to say, "Don't be concerned. I'm not going to marry her."' 'Her' meaning 'them'.

He was, after all, a bachelor who used to patronize the pool at the Rock Hotel, just the sort of place where he would meet girls who might themselves have qualified for a *Vogue* spread. As he pointed out to me, 'I was a bachelor for a long time.' A bachelor who still managed to find time to do some work – often through his 'entertainment' at the Rock Hotel. He enjoyed those jaunts by the pool, but it was proving expensive – £300 each summer, which in 1961 was a lot more money than it is now – and the hotel still costs a lot of money, and the price has increased considerably since then. When it went up to £600, Momy was in a quandary: could he afford that sort of money? So he came up with a possible compromise:

> I went to see the owner, Joe Gaggero, and I said, 'I've just started work. I can't afford to pay you £30, but I'll do a deal with you: you let me in free and every time you want a valuation, I will do it for you – for free.' We shook hands and the deal was done. Since then, I have never once had to pay.

But there have been awkward moments: 'My wife took our grandchildren there, showed our pass and the woman at the door said it was for Mr Solomon Levy himself only. I was furious when I heard about it. I complained, of course, and within an hour there was a pass – "for Solomon Levy and family". All the family.'

It was one of a series of unusual deals. He is still retained as the valuer for a number of churches and religious centres in Gibraltar. He still never charges them a penny. It is not the way to treat religious people, he believes, no matter what that religion is. He is very careful not to use unnecessarily large sledgehammers to crack tiny nuts. One of his clients was to ask him to collect £2 in unpaid rent. He told him to appoint another collector to get hold of the money to cover a few light bulbs. 'I'd rather be a beggar in the street', he says, somewhat dramatically. But that remains one of Momy's great strengths, not just to recall those memories, but to enjoy them at the same time. And enjoy them he certainly does.

But then his favourite way of enjoying himself had to change because of politics. General Franco intervened and closed the frontier with Gibraltar:

> I always say that he was my marriage broker. I couldn't use my MG Midget sports car. I said to myself: 'Well, if they close the frontier, what do I do with the Midget, up the rock, down the rock, around the rock? I better start thinking of tying the knot.' Meanwhile I had been keeping an eye on Sarah. She's ten years younger than I am and I thought she would be the one lady who would become my wife. She had been working in my office part time. So I married her, a local Jewish girl.

THE MARRIED MAN

I don't worry about him.

Sarah Levy

Sarah became the apple of his eye, a beautiful shiny apple, a species that is pretty rare.

A joker of some culture once said, 'Marriage isn't just a word. It's a sentence.' And so it is. But it's a sentence that lucky people are happy to serve. Momy and Sarah Levy are plainly among them.

Momy says that General Francisco Franco was undoubtedly the reason – and he needed something that would serve as a consolation for not being able to use his red Midget. 'Here in Gibraltar, we knew everybody. In any case, Sarah and I are distantly related. Her mother is a second cousin of my father. A previous Solomon Levy, who was a first cousin of my father's, was Sarah's grandfather.' General Franco didn't bother about that. Nor did he know that the breakdown of diplomacy between the Rock and Spain would have such long-lasting consequences. 'The frontier was closed and I said "Right!"'

Certainly, Momy knew Sarah very well: 'We used to go to socials in the youth club. But, as I said, she was ten years younger and I was already doing all sorts of things.' I had gathered as much.

But by the time he became interested in her, Sarah had gone to London and was working in an office. She lived in the north-west suburb of Willesden with three other girls. 'On one of the occasions when she came home, I asked her to come with me to the Rotary dinner.'

He had joined the Rock's Rotary Club, the president of which was the man who would eventually succeed Sir Joshua as Mayor, Abraham Serfaty (another member of the Jewish community), and Momy had become the club's secretary. During this period he had been responsible for the seating plan for their ladies' night: 'I sat two ladies together in the seating plan and they were both wearing the same dress. Did I get it! I said to them, "How was I supposed to know what you were wearing?"'

His dinner with Sarah was more auspicious. 'It wasn't a Jewish occasion, but I heard people say, "Look at Momy. He's with a Jewish girl! He's taking her out. That's it!"'

And it was. The Rotarians, who pride themselves on getting their priorities right, were on the correct lines, even if they didn't know for certain where the track would lead. Momy, however, did:

> I proposed to her. She was going back to England and she said to me, 'I'll think about it.' When she went back to London, she told her housemates, 'Momy has proposed.' They all said, 'I hope you've accepted.' She said, 'I told him I'd think about it.' They all answered: 'Don't be a fool. Write him a letter.' As soon as I received the letter – within twenty-four hours – I got on a plane. I had a ring given to me by my aunt, a very beautiful diamond. I took it to London and had it made in Hatton Garden into a beautiful engagement ring which I gave to her. That was October.

With the ring on Sarah's finger, the young couple set about thinking of where they were to live. His family still owned their block of flats, Carmel House (which had been named after Carmel College: similarity was undoubtedly an asset, which Momy probably thought could also be a good omen) and there was a flat there that they could have. 'So I said, "Don't let's wait too long. Let's get married in January."'

Sarah gave up her job and, as a present, Momy bought her wedding dress for her. 'She came and did all the preparations for the wedding. You should have seen my father's face when I told him we were engaged. Wow! He couldn't believe it. My mother was a little more laid-back. She was the quiet type and kept her feelings more to herself. I could see, however, that my father was over the moon. I remember telling him, "Dad, I'm all right. I'm doing fine."'

Fortunately, Isaac and Rachel also liked Sarah's parents. 'My father said that he would share all the costs. "Whatever Sarah and Momy want, they can have."'

Sarah had to go back to London to collect her belongings. This was a happy journey – so much easier than when she first went to work in London. There was an immigration technicality and she had been barred entry in to the country – and had to fly first to Paris and then back to Gibraltar. Not for the first time, Sir Joshua Hassan, First Minister of Her Majesty's colony of Gibraltar, was brought in to solve the problem. And he did. But not before Sarah had to kick her high heels in the French capital. (In later years, they had trouble getting into San Francisco because their passport wasn't recognized by any of the immigration machines; the problem has since been solved – they now have British passports.)

Three months after the ring was Sarah's, they stood together under a chuppah, the wedding canopy. The year was 1969.

Robert Seruya was the best man. As he told me: 'It was the first time I remember making a speech at a wedding. I was so glad he found the lady who became his wife. It was many, many years before I myself settled down.'

The wedding reception was held in a place that undoubtedly meant the return of old and good memories – the Gibraltar Regiment's officers' mess. 'Out of the 500 people there, only 20 per cent were Jewish. But there was a big family dinner', said Momy. One can only imagine what a Levy family dinner was like. Certainly, it wasn't just the smoked salmon sandwiches which Momy had been used to the last time he had dined in the officers' mess.

The newly-weds went to Israel on honeymoon. But they almost didn't. Other people have nervous reactions to getting married. Momy was deliriously happy, he told me. So his condition once they arrived in London on the stopover point was not due to worries about making the right choice. They booked into the Cumberland Hotel for a wedding night not to be forgotten. He woke up at 1 o'clock with a high temperature. What he said next was not exactly good news for a bride looking forward to visiting a place about which they both knew a lot but which neither had ever visited. 'I'm too ill to go to Israel', he said.

> I then remembered a friend who had been in the Royal Army Medical Corps, a doctor in London, Adrian Fox. I rang him. 'Adrian', I said, 'please come and see me.' So he came and gave me some pills and told me: 'Get out of the country with this cold weather and go to Israel as soon as you can.' So we did just that three days later.

The news of the marriage and the venue for the honeymoon spread around Momy's already greatly expanding social set in Gibraltar. When they arrived in Tel Aviv, the legacy of that Rotary dinner was still very much in their minds – and in other people's, too. The Israeli city's own Rotary group came to what is now Ben Gurion Airport and welcomed them with bunches of flowers. Then they went to a meeting there. How Sarah felt about spending even a small chunk of her honeymoon with a group of Rotarians is not on the record, but it takes little imagination to know that Momy loved it.

What he didn't love was still being on antibiotics. That meant that at first he couldn't sample Israel's wines, which some might have thought was a distinct advantage. Israel had had a wine industry ever since a Lord Rothschild established the first wineries around what is now the city of Rishon Le Tzion (The First in Zion), but its produce was mainly for sacramental purposes; the idea of good table wines – for which the country is now receiving considerable critical acclaim – had not by any means taken root. Momy loved his wine and being unable to have any was a big drawback. There were, of course, other delights about being on honeymoon – and, as he says, he has made up for that one deprivation since.

They stayed at the Kings Hotel in Jerusalem and then went to Tiberius, to visit the tomb of Rabbi Meir Baal Haness. He says they were greeted as honoured guests in the area. Altogether, they were in Israel for two weeks, a lot of the time being introduced to locals as 'the young couple from Gibraltar'.

Today, Sarah is very much the Jewish wife, mother and grandmother. She doesn't talk much about their meeting and believes being romantic is something between her and her ever-loving husband. But she tolerates the way her flat is literally smothered with photographs of Momy with various dignitaries and doesn't care that he is something of a dandy who spends, perhaps – as he accepts – more than he should on his clothes and toys. 'Why not?' she says. 'I do want him to be happy and if this all makes him happy, I am happy too.'

Momy, unlike many men, enjoys shopping: 'In London, I go to the Westfield shopping centre. Or I walk down Piccadilly from one end to the other and if I see something I want, I buy it.'

Shopping in London is, in a way, another of his gestures of love for Britain. Sarah also shares – up to a point, I think – Momy's devotion to that country. She doesn't mind that when he hears 'God Save The Queen' on television he stands up for it in his own living room. She is pleased that he relaxes watching BBC television's political coverage on Sunday mornings. As Momy tells her: 'I was born British, and even if I hadn't been born British, I'd carry on being a subject of

Her Majesty. I would never agree to being Spanish. Nor would I agree if someone suddenly said, "You're Spanish now but you're going to be French."' No. There's no doubt where Momy's heart lies – most of it, of course, with Sarah.

The Levy family eventually expanded to have twenty-odd grandchildren; the number tends to increase so regularly that giving a number here will prove to be a fruitless exercise, as it will surely be out of date once the book reaches the shop shelves. But not Momy's love for them all. 'My family is my fortune', he says again and again.

In a way, Gibraltar benefits from Momy's devotion to his family and to all the other causes that have enveloped him like a warm overcoat on one of the occasional winter days that even the Rock experiences. It benefits in the way that perhaps only a very small place can, in deriving satisfaction from the devotion of one of its citizens. The population respects a man who cares, and since everybody does really know everybody else, his caring personality is as well known as are his bow tie and bowler hat as he walks to synagogue on Shabbat. That really is no small thing and it is undoubtedly why practically everything he does finds itself in the pages of the *Gibraltar Chronicle*. Sarah probably basks in his reflected glory, but keeps it very much to herself. People don't recognize her the way they do Momy, and if they did she would probably hate it. He himself, of course, knows just how fortunate he is:

> And I always say to myself, 'Thank God, I have done something with this life and you've paid me the way you have.' And you know, starting with my parents and then getting married and all that has been a wonderful thing. I pray for all of them, one by one. Sometimes, we take it all for granted and then, you know, we don't realize how lucky we have been.

THE IN-BETWEEN YEARS

We are a strong family. We have our differences, but we always stick together.

James Levy

The 1980s and 1990s were years of quiet consolidation. Momy's marriage was proving to be idyllic. His children were starting to get married; the first grandchildren came. He had been president of his synagogue since 1975 (a position he still has) and then of the community as head of the Jewish Management Board for three years between 1996 and 1999. And he carried on doing his good works.

Momy was very much involved in the Chamber of Commerce. In fact, he was very much involved in the business community of his home town, period. For twenty-five years he served as a member of the Trade Licensing Committee. People wanting to establish themselves as business men or women on the Rock had first to get a licence from the committee. He had to be elected to this organization, and that was in itself a tribute to the work that he was doing in local commercial life.

As an ex-serviceman, he made sure that his fellow members of the Royal British Legion carried on doing their duty to Queen and country, and, at the annual Jewish Remembrance parade and service in Whitehall, the ever-immaculate Solomon Levy marched behind the sign that said 'Gibraltar'. He regarded it as a great opportunity to fly the flag not only of the Rock, but also of its Jewish community.

There are, of course, two points to these services, always held on the Sunday after the main Remembrance commemoration at the same place: one, an opportunity to say the Kaddish, the Jewish memorial prayer; two, to show the immense Jewish contribution to the war effort. Momy was there to do both things – at first in his Gibraltar Regiment uniform, and then wearing the bowler hat and overcoat probably more smartly than anyone else on parade, and taking off that hat in salute as he walked past the famous war memorial, the Cenotaph.

As for the Legion, as we have seen, he willingly surrendered his office of president so that an older man could take on the role and himself became chairman.

It will not come as any surprise that he was a member of the Gibraltar Association. If it had not existed, he would have been a one-man Gibraltar Association himself without any trouble.

Then there was the health of the people among whom he lived. Or perhaps, rather, the bad health of some people. He once had a meeting with the chaplain of the local King's Chapel, attached to the Governor's residence. 'Mr Levy', the man said, 'we want to form a society for cancer relief. Would you join the committee?' 'I'd be delighted', Momy replied. He loved committees, of course, almost as other people love certain sports. But there's no question that he did believe in the cause. Before long, they had built a hospice and raised thousands of pounds to buy equipment and pay for the services of specialists. The hospice was named, at Momy's suggestion, after the Governor's wife, Lady Williams, whose idea it was in the first place.

Momy organized functions in aid of the cause: 'I wanted to run a ball in Gibraltar to raise money for the cause. The Governor said, "Momy, the Convent is yours."' The evening raised £8,000 for cancer relief funds.

He was made, and still is, a member of the Gibraltar Blind Society. Appropriately, he was made a charity commissioner, too.

His association with the Rotary movement was cemented when he was made president of the Gibraltar Rotary Club.

Housing was also a big necessity in promoting health in Gibraltar. After years of apparent stagnation, building-work projects were announced and were put into operation. Momy lobbied the government, wrote letters and insisted that priority should be given to local families. 'We must build houses for Gibraltarians first and then for the English people who want to live here', he declared.

There were other organizations on which he put his stamp. For ten years, he was chairman of the Gibraltar Music Centre.

The Chief Minister, Peter Caruana, regarded Momy as a particularly irritating thorn in his flesh. 'Within twenty-four hours, I had a letter from him informing me, "As from now you are not a member of the Trade Licensing committee."'

It was one of the few disappointments of those years. More significant in his life were the family events and what he, his mother and his siblings regarded at the time as the big tragedy in their lives: in 1974 his father died. Momy said he didn't think he could survive without the senior Isaac Levy in his life.

There was the usual Jewish funeral – the body wrapped in a shroud as the three brothers lowered it into the six-foot-deep grave. Afterwards, they hugged each other, promising a lifetime of love, which each has honoured to the letter in the years since.

'I was damned scared that day', Momy remembers. 'But then when Abraham and I had together laid the body in the grave, I felt ... I won't say satisfaction, but I had the feeling of being with him to the very end, a man who was so important in my life.' I wondered why until that moment he had felt 'scared'. 'Because', he told me, 'I was scared of seeing somebody go.' Since then, he has been on the rota of members of the Jewish community who remain with bodies for up to twenty-four hours from death to burial: 'Not for one moment is the person left alone until he is buried.' When a woman dies, Sarah performs the ancient ritual of *tahara*, the cleansing of the body.

'They say time is a great healer', Momy said. 'After thirteen months, you realize you have to make the most of it.'

His mother died in 1987 when Momy was 50. Rachel had been ill for some time, and the brothers Momy and James embarked on a demonstration of filial love that could make a chapter in a novel:

> My mother lived in a flat with two floors. She didn't want to move, although it was very inconvenient for her. The family home at 5 Governor's Lane was where all her children had been born, and leaving would have been far too painful. So for a couple of years, James and I used to meet every day at six. And we used to carry our mother up two floors and used to take her to her door and then have a cup of tea with her and a chat. When we left, one or two of our children would come – so that she'd never be left alone.

Rachel Levy had been left financially very stable, thanks to a family inheritance. She was determined to hold on to it. James recalled her telling her children: 'You can have whatever you want, but I will hold on to [the money that formed part of] the inheritance. I'm not going to be like my mother and be dependent on my children.' They told her that the way to avoid big death duties – or inheritance tax, as it became – was to make over gifts to her children:

> We told her that everything was for her and for her life. And the rest, afterwards was for her children. It wasn't actually so, because it would affect the scheme. My mother wasn't a woman of business, but we made her chairman of the company we had set up and all the assets of our property portfolio would go into the company. So she was very comfortable. I made her sign a number of minutes and she was very happy. The property was

> actually in our name but she lived for fifteen years after our father and never knew that it wasn't really hers.
>
> She used to tell James: 'Go to your brother and give him £2,000 to have a holiday. He hasn't had one for a while.' So she felt everything was hers and the five of us pretended for fifteen years. Every penny that was needed went to her and only if anything was left did we pay it to ourselves.

Momy signed everything.

It was probably because of that family thing that Sarah and Momy decided that their son Isaac should follow his father into Carmel College, now with Kopul Rosen's son, Jeremy, as head. After Isaac's grandfather died, a decision was made that he should go and live with his grandmother. The entry into Carmel was by way of being something of a shock. Nevertheless, he told me that he enjoyed the experience almost as much as his father appreciated the sense of continuity that his enrolment in the Levy alma mater gave him.

They have always had a particularly strong bond, a father-son relationship to be envied. Only once was the younger Levy subjected to corporal punishment at home: 'That was the only time I ever smacked him', Momy said. 'Afterwards, I apologized. I said, "Please forgive me."' It takes a particularly loving father to do that. Isaac told me how much he appreciated it. Certainly, he says, he didn't believe he could go on offending with impunity.

Isaac, who now works on his own account as a corporate finance specialist, says of his time at Carmel: 'It did me a lot of good. Going to boarding school makes you very independent.' But he said that he did feel homesick:

> My father would ask me every week, 'Do you want to come home? Would you like to come back?' That was a safety valve that made life there more manageable. I had a mixture of self-confidence

> and feeling reserved. I suppose I was a little shy. My father could relate to my experience because he had been at the school, too. In fact, there were some teachers who remembered him.

The father remained proud of the son when the headmaster told him how well Isaac was doing. Momy could only think of the number of times he had had to 'tick off' Jeremy when he himself was a prefect.

Teachers at the school would surely remember Isaac, too, if only the school had stayed in business. He left Carmel College as head boy. Momy says: 'The first thing I did when Isaac became head boy was to bring him a Gibraltar flag which he put outside his study. Jeremy Rosen told me he was the best head boy he could remember.'

After Carmel, Isaac went to Cambridge. As his father said: 'Since the age of 12, he has hardly lived in Gibraltar.'

Some of those teachers might even have remembered Momy's love for that Spanish 'Gilbert and Sullivan' art form, zarzuela. He was a great supporter of the Zarzuela Association, which still meets at the Instituto de Cervantes, a place where Spanish lessons are given. Proof, if proof were needed, that Gibraltar's determination to stay British does not extend to hatred for Spain, its people or its culture. Of course, it was also a chance for Momy to exercise one of his great passions, music in all its forms. If it could be combined with a Jewish element, he was a happy man indeed. In 1992, Momy joined in a commemoration to mark the 500th anniversary of the expulsion of the Jews from Spain – and, more important, their *official* welcome back from the government and the lifting of the *unofficial* ban on Jews visiting the country, which some sources say had been imposed by the rabbinate (although the theory of there being a *cherem* or excommunication on any Jew who did go there has been disputed). He went to Toledo, site of an ancient synagogue which became a church. The Israel Philharmonic, conducted by Zubin Mehta, played at the concert, which was attended by the Queen of Spain.

On this occasion, every Jew with the name Toledano was given the key to the city. An interesting point: Dayan Pinchas Toledano was the rival of Rabbi Abraham Levy when both sought the spiritual leadership of the Spanish and Portuguese congregation in London. In the end a compromise was worked out that both accepted.

In 1999, Momy's love of Britain reached its apogee. He went to Buckingham Palace again, this time on his own account, to receive his MBE. What he says about that time when he wore a morning coat and top hat in his own right is so typically Solomon Levy: 'I was fortunate that the day for my investiture was actually my birthday. There were choices of dates when I could have received my medal, so of course I chose my birthday.' Her Majesty was kind to him as she pinned the medal to his chest (or at least to the part of his coat that was close to his chest); she smiled, and Momy broke court etiquette which decreed that mere commoners, even those who are called Levy, do not speak until spoken to: 'I said, "Forty-three years ago, I was sitting in the second row watching my uncle get a medal." "Who was your uncle?" she asked. "Sir Joshua Hassan", he answered. "Ah yes", said the Queen, "I remember him well".'

That was not quite the end of the story. This is how he describes the second episode of his relationship with Elizabeth II: 'I had an MP friend (who became a member of the House of Lords) who rang me and invited me the very next day after my investiture to go with him to the palace because his wife couldn't manage it.' Again he breached protocol. It was a drinks party and Momy, as is his wont, approached the Queen: 'She gave me a look that said, "Oh no, not you again."' He is certain she recognized him. But he had a question to ask: 'Mam. It would be the dream of your Gibraltarian subjects if you were to visit us for the Millennium.'

The Queen was not in a promising mood (and indeed the visit never happened). 'Look what happened last time I was there', she said. 'What will my cousin [the King of Spain] say? Last time, they closed the frontier.' Momy, of course, had an answer: 'Ma'am', he said, 'with all due respect to His Majesty the King of Spain, the Rock of Gibraltar belongs to her Majesty the Queen.' As he said, 'I bowed and left.'

Even that wasn't quite the end of this story. A week later, the Queen visited the Mansion House, the home of the Lord Mayor of London. At that time, the Lord Mayor was the Jewish Lord Levine. He had appointed as his chaplain a certain Rabbi Abraham Levy from Gibraltar. He was introduced. The Queen told him that the previous week she had met a chap who had tried to persuade her to go to Gibraltar. 'That's my brother', said Abraham. She replied, 'You seem to be everywhere'.

It was all very theatrical. That is not to say that his visits to the palace were the only theatrical experiences of his life – after those in his childhood, that is. In 1980, he joined the local Trafalgar Drama Group for their amateur production of *Fiddler on the Roof*:

> I heard that they were putting on the show and so I went up to a man called Leslie who was producing it – his wife succeeded me as mayor – I said, 'I'd like to be in the show. How about me playing the rabbi?' So he looks at me and I said, 'I'm made to measure for this part. I've got my brother and three brothers-in-law who are rabbis. Please give me the part.' He replied that he'd give me a chance – if I promised to go to rehearsal – 'but you have to behave yourself'. He thought I had the reputation for being all over the place. He saw me, I asked him to give me a trial and then he gave me the part. I started to go to rehearsals and grow a longer beard. I was younger then, so I had to put talcum powder on my hair and beard. Anyway, the time comes along and we go on stage – the show had been scheduled for the Monday, Tuesday, Wednesday,

> Thursday and Friday. The Friday performance was, of course, cancelled because of Shabbat.

But another was held on Saturday – once the Sabbath had 'gone out'.

Momy was delighted, a wonderful opportunity to show off – officially. He sent news of his new 'career' to the family. To his sister Loli, the wife of a rabbi, living in the *frum* London suburb of Golders Green, he sent an appeal: could she find a hat similar to the one that the spiritual leader of Anatevka might have worn? 'She sent me one.' It was just one of the things about entering the world of the thespian that he enjoyed: 'Yes, for five nights, I really did feel I was a rabbi. And I could dance and sing. The army provided a four-piece band. I must say, it worked out beautifully.'

The great and the good in Gibraltar (as if everyone in Gibraltar was not both great and good in Solomon Levy's book) were there. A rear admiral who was the commander of the forces on the Rock went on stage to praise the participants. And he added: 'Momy, if I hadn't seen it, I would never have believed it.'

As Momy proved time and again, observing Jewish life was never going to hamper his progress in pubic life. And that public life was about to become even more prominent than he had ever imagined.

MR MAYOR

The greatest moment in my life.

Solomon Levy

The news came as a total surprise. When Momy left the office of the Chief Minister, he probably whooped with joy – he really can't remember. What he can recall, with the sense of a historian telling of a major political or military event, is that he could have been no happier had he just been told he had won a fortune on the lottery, or if one of his children had been given a peerage. For Momy Levy, on that day in May 2008, it was all those things. In a way, the peerage was his. Well, not quite a peerage. He was being offered a job for the following August which he would have craved if only he had known it was becoming available – the position of Mayor of Gibraltar.

Of course, he accepted. In a way, it was the fulfilment of all his dreams. It was formalizing all the things he had done, virtually unsung, despite the jokes about him running to the *Gibraltar Chronicle* every time he went for a walk. He had done a very great deal without anyone knowing about it, for his city/town/country and for its Jewish community. It was saying what so many others – perhaps more Ashkenazim than Sephardim – would announce: this is a *mensch*. It is a word that means so much more than, literally, a man. It's a very special man. No one could take that away from him.

Naturally, it would give him a chance to wear one or two new suits – try and stop him – but over them he would don the blue-and-gold robes that his uncle, the famous and iconic Sir Joshua Hassan, had worn. Even more important, the gold chain that went with the ensemble. But none of that should take away the real significant feature of the honour which was about to be given to him. To be walking in Sir Joshua's footsteps, as well as to wear his robes, was one thing. But the fact of his appointment was very much another. He wasn't just going to be mayor. He would be the first 'Civil Mayor', the first who was appointed because he was simply a worthy citizen. Not a politician – although he had, as we have seen, his political views which didn't exactly coincide with those of the governing Gibraltar Social Democrat Party. But they supported the idea of his appointment. No, for the first time the honour was going to a man who wasn't and had never been a member of the Gibraltar council or the parliament. As he said:

> In 2002, the Chief Minister, Peter Caruana, changed the constitution to allow that. He told me: 'From now on, the Mayor will be a civil position, nothing to do with politics, and his sole job would be to receive VIP visitors to Gibraltar who would go and call on the mayor in the mayor's parlour. And he will give parties to different organizations. You have been proposed by the government with the approval of the opposition.'

All his work in an entirely unofficial capacity had been noted.

It turned out that the ten ministers in the Cabinet had been going over a list of the names of people who would possibly be suited to the job: 'In the Cabinet I had four members who were very friendly towards me. But I didn't know they'd be friendly to that extent. Apparently, they chose me and Caruana said, "Fine, I agree."'

The idea was that there would also be a deputy mayor who would take over the job the following year, which was the British pattern: 'I was the first, so I hadn't been deputy to anyone.' If anything, that made the job even sweeter. Momy continued:

> When I first became mayor, the Chief Minister said, 'From now on, no politics', and it was going to apply to National Day on 10th September. This, too, would be different from before. Then, the Chief Minister would give a speech, the Leader of the Opposition would give a speech, Members of Parliament would give a speech. It was a very political thing. I think the Chief Minister's idea was to keep shalom with the Spaniards. So he decided that there will be a proclamation about what we Gibraltarians want. The mayor will come to the balcony in the Piazza. At the end, we'll say, 'Release the balloons.' Which made a difference from certain countries where new leaders might shout, 'Release the political prisoners.' No. Nothing like that in Gibraltar.

In August 2008 he was sworn in: 'There was a ceremony in the mayor's parlour and all the local VIPs came. Caruana made a speech and then I went out of the room with him – and I came back in with my robes on. The outgoing mayor then put the chain on me.' Even now, Momy still savours the day and the ceremony.

It 'didn't cost much', says Momy reflectively – frequently the be-all and end-all of mayoral politics in the civic world. 'I was given the proclamation and read it to myself a few times a couple of days before, and thought, "God, this is a dead thing. No way!"' And no way it was. Four thousand people gathered in the Piazza. He added a few personal touches, mentioned his uncle Sir Joshua, and ended with three words repeated three times (not mentioned at all in the written script): 'God bless Gibraltar.' Then, in his mayoral robes – which made a change from his bowler hat or the colourful waistcoat – he walked down : 'I shook hands with every man and kissed every woman.' His rabbi might not have approved, but his 'subjects' did. As they would a hundred times afterwards. And as they would a hundred times, too, they called out, 'Momy! Momy! Momy!'

He has no regrets about the way he did things – certainly not about kissing the women: 'As they say in Spanish, "that touch wasn't in the programme".'

Needless to say, he took to the job like a boy footballer who suddenly realizes he has been made a striker for a Premier League side.

He was given £14,000 to cover expenses for his year in office, which turned out to be – as he knew it would be – not enough:

> Towards the end of my term, my PA, Andrew Rowbottom – a wonderfully helpful man who organized me; wherever he told me to go, I went – said I had spent £22,000. I told him not to worry. The Chief Minister called me and said, 'You do realize, don't you, that you have overspent.' I told him, 'Look, you are always saying that our economy in Gibraltar is very flamboyant. What is £8,000 to do what I managed to do?' Even now, people say that a year was too little. I should have stayed for four or five years.

He is particularly proud that the first VIP guest he entertained in that parlour which for twelve months would be his was the then Israeli Ambassador, Ronnie Prosser.

His entertaining wasn't exclusively for important people. He gave a party for the local taxi drivers, 'who took people to and from City Hall every day of the week but had never been inside. I wasn't sure if the Chief Minister was very pleased about that. The cabbies loved Momy, and presented him with a gift that was made-to-measure for his favourite off-duty habit – a box of cigars: 'I used to love cigars, but then I got cancer and had to stop.' The partying went on, however, before that disease was diagnosed. The taxi drivers would offer their mayor anything they had in their power to give. But he wasn't taking: 'Now, I tell them – and they all know me – I want a taxi. But I am paying. Otherwise don't come ... I gave parties for the elderly, and for the handicapped. I gave one for the contestants for Miss

Gibraltar.' Momy enjoyed that, as he did almost every duty he performed as the Rock's leading citizen.

When he took the salute at a parade by the Royal Gibraltar Regiment, he was the one standing on the platform: 'The Chief Minister was on the pavement below.' Momy loves to tell that story. And that's not in the least surprising. This was his own old regiment celebrating their 70th anniversary surrounded by all the top brass around: 'There were a lot of colonels there and here I was, a mere captain in the reserve, taking the salute. Of course, I loved that.' So much so that he commissioned a painting of the event which he presented to the Regiment's new officers' mess. A copy now hangs in Momy's office.

He constantly loved to draw parallels with his uncle – the man he is seen saluting in yet another of the pictures in his office of a young moustachioed officer looking admiringly at the man whose robes he now wore himself. But because he wasn't a politician (officially) he wouldn't scale the same heights: 'No, don't forget he was also Chief Minister. He got his CBE and three knighthoods, including the one I like best to talk about, the KCMG [Knight Commander of the Order of St Michael and St George] which stood for "Kindly Call Me God."'There were people who thought Momy himself was capable of a miracle or two, so he never needed to ask them to call him God.

Talking of which, he never abandoned his work for the Jewish community, who wouldn't have called any human being God. Nor did he experience any of the anti-Semitism which just occasionally his uncle suffered, with cries of 'Go back to Israel'. The average Gibraltarians liked having him among themselves. Rightly, he was seen as no different from any of his fellow citizens.

He also fostered the usual (for him, that is) interfaith relations. The man who once went to Rome to see the local Catholic priest made up to a bishop couldn't have been expected to do anything less: 'I knew that the Pope would wear a white *kippah*, so I wore a black one because I was given a place of honour in the VIP seats – along with my morning coat.' (The tailcoat could not be ignored or forgotten.) 'I must say that the Catholics here were very impressed that Sarah and I went to Rome specially to witness that.' He himself revelled in the speech made by the Irish-born bishop. 'Ladies and gentlemen we now have the white Pope and the black Pope'. No one can be sure whether John Paul II heard that. Most people in Gibraltar did – as they heard about practically everything he did. Like Momy's contribution to the menswear industry. He decided that it was all very well, the then Governor putting up a Gibraltar flag outside his residence, but there needed to be something that other people could do to commemorate their links with both the Rock and Britain. So he designed a tie, an accessory in warm red, bearing crossed flags – the Union flag and the red-and-white Gibraltar ensign with its castle emblem in the centre. He himself usually wore his trademark bow tie, but the crossed flags wouldn't have worked on a bow. 'I usually only wear a tie on special occasions.' He told me:

> I wrote to the manufacturer on my estate agent notepaper and the fellow in charge, accepting the order, wrote as a PS, 'Excuse me for asking, but you're an estate agent, why are you ordering three dozen ties?' The Governor was impressed. He said, 'You know, Momy, that was a very good idea that shows how close are our ties [no pun probably, just probably, intended] are with Britain.

Of course, Momy didn't need to be told that. To this day, he presents a tie to all the dignitaries who come his way – and they still do come his way. At the last count, the three dozen has become close to 400.

Ties went to the leading figures in Spain's border town of La Linea, too, which Momy saw as a gesture of friendship and not a compromise on international politics:

> Locally, there's a patron saint, the Lady of Europa. People here made a figure, a very nice figure, to present to La Linea. So I rang the Bishop – I called him 'Father' because he didn't like to be called Bishop, this man, Bishop Caruana, a man who was really something special – and asked him what time the procession would be.
>
> 'What do you want to know for?' he asked. 'Why do you ask?' I replied. 'Because', he said, 'you are Jewish.' That wasn't a good enough answer for me. I told him, 'I'm the Mayor of Gibraltar and therefore I have to represent my town.' So he said, 'That's very nice of you.' What I didn't realize was that the church was so damn far away from the border, we had to walk miles. I was worn out by the time I got there. The Bishop of La Linea was there to welcome us – and I think a lot of other bishops, too. It was an important Catholic occasion. I must say I felt a bit odd, but then when I met the Mayor of La Linea we started talking about bullfighting – which is very popular in his town. We got on wonderfully and I felt a lot better. You know, though, for weeks and weeks after that procession, the whole of Gibraltar was talking about how this mayor had joined the procession. After all, I wasn't *asked* to go.

Another of those memories that have led to a regular pattern. As he told me:

> Whenever there is a service in the church, I'm the one who represents the Jewish community because no one else will go and I believe we should be represented. My brother James is invited as president of the community when the Governor is present at a service, and he sends me on his behalf.
>
> When they say Mass, there comes a time when they all shake hands and say 'Peace be upon you.' But they come to me and say, 'Shalom, shalom.' I like that very much.

The visit to La Linea made an impression for another reason. The man who so frequently crossed the border in his red MG Midget – and still does, usually on foot now that the MG has long since died the death inevitable for sports cars – for the first time went without having to show a passport or any other form of ID. It reminded me of the time Ernest Bevin, not a fan of Momy's people, it has to be said, was asked what he liked best about being Foreign Secretary. He replied, in his gruff West Country accent, 'to go to Waterloo station and get on a bloody train without buying a ticket'.

Momy won't say that travelling without ID was the best part of being in the highest echelons of Gibraltar life. It wasn't even when he received the MBE from the Queen – not as a guest at another's big event, but at his own investiture for services to Gibraltar, for being mayor, for serving in the army for eighteen years and for his work on various committees. 'It was very nice to receive it, but being mayor ... that was really special. I'd rather have been mayor than be knighted.'

It gave him an opportunity to recognize other people's contributions to life on the Rock, as well. 'I gave the freedom of the city to the Boy Scouts', he recalled. As I have said, 'I'd been a scout myself, when we used to have those round hats, like the ones the American army wore in the First World War. They knew how much I liked those hats, so they dressed five boys who stood next to me wearing them when I took the salute in the Piazza.'

Then there was the visit to Madeira when the island was twinned with Gibraltar. That was an event close to Momy's heart – even the speech he had to make in Portuguese. He was taken to see his old house and even the theatre where he had taken part in little amateur plays. He was reminded he was a show-off even in those days.

The parties he gave may initially have given the local caterers moments of pause. The food had to be kosher, so he brought in his own suppliers: 'Whenever there are functions which Jewish people attend, the council calls my daughter to supply kosher canapés and wine.' When the kosher caterer was not called in, Momy would find a way to manage: 'I would have a boiled egg, smoked salmon and other fish. It wasn't a meal. Just a tiny tapas. But I'd mix up my guests – Protestants, Catholics and Jews altogether.'

Not surprisingly, Sarah didn't take much to the role of wife of the mayor: 'She was very shy. She didn't come to many functions.' Some she did go to. There were visits from ships' captains which were important, and the visit from the Mayor of La Linea, to say nothing of a group of army chaplains. And, of course, there was the Israeli ambassador's arrival – which Momy had been planning before he achieved his big opportunity, the dream of a lifetime which he had never really planned.

There was nothing that was going to spoil their marriage, however. He and Sarah remained as close as ever. But her absence from civic functions didn't inhibit Momy. It was all going so well – until the day he attended the Royal Salute at Edinburgh Castle by the Royal Gibraltar Regiment. He hadn't been feeling too good and had lost his appetite, which really should have caused this keen meat-eater to be extra concerned. But in Edinburgh he was not feeling well at all: 'I wasn't eating properly, but I didn't pay much attention to that. But once in Scotland, I felt very, very ill. I thought I was going to die.' As he said: 'I went all dizzy, yellow and stuff. A friend said to me, "Are you feeling well?" Well, I wasn't. So the next day, I flew back to Gibraltar. I was OK then. I was able to fly.' When he got home, the commanding officer of the regiment, who was attending a function with him, came to his aid. 'Take him straight away to a doctor', he ordered. 'Take my car. I'll get another one.'

The doctor took it very seriously. He ordered Momy to hospital:

> He knew it was cancer. He told Sarah, 'There's no decision to be made. Either he has an operation or you don't have a husband.' Within hours I was in hospital in Torremolinos.

> I was with a doctor there for two hours. He said, 'Mr Levy, a cancerous tumour in your colon has been diagnosed. You will not leave the clinic. If you had left it for another week, it would have burst and you would be dead.' Every morning I thank God that I am here to tell the story and that I must have done something good because I've got Sarah as my wife.
>
> The operation cost the equivalent of £15,000. The Gibraltar Health Authority would not pay me a penny – because the operation was in Spain. Had it been in the UK, they would have paid up. I was in Spain there for three weeks. Sarah never left my side for three weeks.

The old Momy Levy propensities came into force:

> The last week that I was there, we had a beautiful nurse there. She had a gorgeous figure. I told her, 'Miss, I hope you don't mind, but as Mayor of Gibraltar, I'm going to name you Miss Torremolinos, because you really are A1.' She rushed out of the room, telling people, 'The Mayor of Gibraltar has named me Miss Toremolinos.'

That was probably the first time that Momy had really come back to being himself. 'Every evening, the surgeon came to see me. He used to call me "Don Solomon" and he said, "Don Solomon, we love you here. You're a good patient. But please don't spoil my nurses." When I left, I went back to being mayor and gave three more parties. So, thank God, I was able to fulfil my year.'

He had to have chemotherapy after his operation, which he said affected his memory to an extent, but not enough to make interviews for this book difficult. 'I went to see a Harley Street neurologist, who told me, "I'm afraid, sir, the chemo has affected a nerve in your brain." I told him, "Excuse me. I haven't got a brain."' One of the effects of the drugs, however, has been that at certain times of the evening he loses contact with his feet. Not such a silly statement as it sounds: 'At half past nine or a quarter to ten, I can't feel them. We were in London one night and my wife said to me, "Take your feet away. They're very cold." I said, "I'm sorry, darling, I can't feel them."'

The support he got from local people didn't surprise him. Friends and strangers wrote to him or telephoned. Christians told him, 'Momy, we're praying for you.' 'My Jewish friends all said prayers, too.'

He put an advertisement in the *Gibraltar Chronicle*:

> I wanted to thank all my friends, Jews and non-Jews for their prayers, I said. And I added that that was much more important to me than all the medicines I was having. To this day, I appreciate the way people still call me 'Mr Mayor'. I said, 'Don't call me that.' But they tell me, 'To me, you'll always be the mayor.'

And actually an 'honourable mayor'. The chain of office bears the names of every mayor who has worn it. When the office was a political appointment, the mayors had the title 'The Honourable'. So when Momy's name was inscribed, he, too, was inscribed as 'The Honourable Solomon Levy.' But when a future mayor was installed, he was told that he wasn't entitled to the two words that Momy liked so much. No mayor in England – and this was given the same status as far as mayor was concerned – was called 'The Honourable', which in Gibraltar's case was a political designation. Nobody has suggested erasing the title from the chain. As if they'd dare. But even if it was never official, that has always been the way his fellow Gibraltarians regarded Momy.

It was, after all, during his mayoralty that he came up with the idea that has since for ever linked the name Solomon Levy with Gibraltar's own self-pride: the celebration of National Day and its red-and-white theme with which this book practically began. It not only illustrated Momy's commitment to Gibraltar, but was his own way of showing how people can get on, even when their political affiliations are totally different.

Indeed, despite all his efforts to make sure that the world knows about Gibraltar and his political antipathy to Spanish ambitions, he joined a society based in the neighbouring country, aimed at achieving good relations between Gibraltar and Spain. He has invited Spaniards not only to walk down Main Street, but to see the Rock's synagogues, too – on consideration, an important development which seemed to merge Momy's two passions, Gibraltar and its Jewish community.

He has government approval for much of this:

> Sometimes, the MoD ask me to show various people round the synagogues. And the first thing they say to me is, 'Why this business of men downstairs and women upstairs? Surely, we're all the same and should be treated as the same?' I answer them [by] saying two things. 'Firstly, I might have a beard, but I'm not a rabbi. But I come to synagogue, and when I come to synagogue I come to concentrate, to pray. If I had a luscious blonde sitting next to me, I couldn't do that.'

A man of conscience who knows about what others might consider his weaknesses. But in a public figure it is surely a strength of character – realizing that changing his personality could never be on the level – and no one has ever charged him with doing that.

His serious statement gave way to the inevitable joke which everyone who ever goes to an all-day service on Yom Kippur will remember: the rabbi who said that mixed seating would never work because his sermons would inevitably lead to men and women sleeping together. His sense of humour transcends language: 'I once went to a Spanish gathering and was introduced to a couple of Catholic priests.' He started to speak in their own language and apologized for what might be coming. One of them interrupted: 'Don't worry, son. Honest, don't worry. But in future, I will tell the jokes.'

The Gibraltar Regiment didn't do much in the way of joking. They remembered the record number of 175-gun salutes, and presented him, as mayor, with an inscribed shell. It is, as might be expected, on show in the somewhat crowded Momy Levy office.

What that office would have been like without Momy as mayor is a reasonable subject for conjecture. But what Momy would have been like, had he not had the title that went with the robes, and the chain that awards him the title of 'The Honourable', is easier to think about. We don't need the details to realize that his life was changed for ever. His personality, however, certainly was not.

NORMALITY

Without him, this would be a very different place. Everybody knows him. Everybody talks to him.

Joe Garcia

When he was no longer mayor, it was very much a question of getting back to normality – whatever that was. He said that people still called him 'Mr Mayor'. Perhaps to put them right he has had a T-shirt made inscribed with the legend: 'I used to be Mayor of Gibraltar'. If they did still call him Mayor it was as much out of respect as of benign ignorance. If it was good enough for Bill Clinton still to be called 'Mr President', why couldn't Solomon Levy still be called by his old title? It was almost as if he were entitled to it by right.

It took time for recovery from the debilitating and unanticipated illness, but he coped, as far as the public were concerned – even if he and his family were not really feeling that way – as if nothing had happened. Apart from being Gibraltar's first citizen, that is.

On 25 October 2011, Momy celebrated his seventy-fifth birthday in true Levy style. There was a banquet for all the people with whom he had had contact, both privately and in business and community work, Jew and non-Jew. Among those was the Governor, Sir Adrian Johns, who gave a speech in praise of his friend: 'I remarked, "he told me that this was only the first of his birthday celebrations. The second would be on his Jewish birthday, the third would be a family party. [I said that] even the Queen has only two birthdays, so Momy had got one up again."'

People have been assessing his position in Gibraltar society ever since. Joe Garcia, editor of one of the Rock's daily newspapers, *Panorama*, said: 'He's a character, you know. He's used to promoting Gibraltar. It's never a case of him doing something one day and then people forgetting about it the next. You don't forget him or what he did.'

Momy himself occasionally turns his mind to philosophizing about his life and his future. He told me:

> I know if I stopped working, within a week, I'd be an old man. So long as what I do works, I'll continue. But if I get ill, I'd want to go. I don't want to be a bother to anyone. There's nothing worse than seeing people around you worrying about you. For them, it's a shock, but for the person who goes, it's a blessing.

But he doesn't intend to allow that to happen. It's not one of the blessings he makes on Friday nights, that's for sure.

Those Sabbath meals were occasions for Momy to enjoy his food tremendously. Now, there is a limit to how much he can consume. 'But I have to eat regularly, which means I can't fast on Yom Kippur, which was a big change to my lifestyle. I still need my meat and my wine.'

And he still wants his Queen. Just before the Diamond Jubilee of 2012, Momy made his big move, and his public demonstration of loyalty: 'I had got the idea in November 2011. So I said to myself ...'. Another Momy soliloquy was coming:

> I said to myself, I'm going to hang a banner outside my office. But the Parliament said to me, 'I'm afraid you have to ask for planning permission.' I applied and got a 'No'. It was, they said, too big. I was setting a precedent and – hold on – it was in the wrong area.

> Facing the Convent. Where better place could there be, a picture of Her Majesty with the message 'God save the Queen'? It seemed ridiculous.

He has a theory about why it was turned down. There were people who did not want to upset their Spanish VIP visitors, who might take exception when they visited the Governor or Chief Minister. He followed James's advice to appeal. 'James said, "Before we appeal, we should have a petition."' A petition was drawn up and 2,800 people signed it: 'People were queuing up to sign it.'

Just then, the Chief Minister and government changed. Momy was told by the new Government to reapply to the Planning Committee. An agreement was reached. He could have planning permission for a year only – Diamond Jubilee Year.

The remaining question was where it should go – outside the parliament or in Main Street. Momy had no doubt: 'The Queen is the mother of parliaments [adapting the phrase usually given to the Westminster parliament] so it should go facing the parliament – outside my office.' And for all of 2012, there it was placed, with the Queen in glorious yellow. He loves yellow, even if it could have been responsible for his bank account going red. But, of course, it didn't – even if the banner did cost him £2,000. He is convinced it was money well spent. Every day he takes lunch outside his daughter Kelly's restaurant when, as we noted, he cannot get through a meal without being stopped to talk, just as a fork is about to reach his mouth. Now, these people had something else to interest them: 'One after the other, they'd come to take photographs – of my banner.'

The Queen was one thing. His loyalty to his Jewish roots was another, and nothing would shake that link from him, either. When AJEX, the British Association of Jewish Ex-Servicemen and Women, journeyed to Paris on a let's-gets-together trip, he went along with them and witnessed the laying of a wreath. He also found opportunities to talk to a French general there, to show his own solidarity with his Jewish countrymen who were war and Occupation veterans.

There was one other thing he was able to do – buy some French model soldiers. Not doing something like that would be to ask him to change his whole personality and no one would ask or expect him to do that. His personality has permeated his family totally. The fact that it exists among the Levys is as much due to Momy himself as anything else. As he told me, 'I'm a great believer in keeping in touch. When my children married and went to live abroad – one daughter to Israel and then to Palo Alto in California – we'd go and visit twice a year.

His son Isaac, whose home is in London, says: 'My parents have always made me feel contented. Being brought up in this sort of family makes you feel very enclosed. You don't have to prove anything to anyone.'

Momy must feel the same way. He has no money worries. 'I'm not poor', he agrees, but adds, 'I'm not a millionaire. My fortune is in Gibraltar – my family. But I also have a flat, an office. Otherwise, I haven't a penny to my name. I spend it as I earn it. I don't know how long I'm going to last, so while I am here I'm going to enjoy it.'

If this were a trial and the question of calling witnesses came up, most if not all would testify to the same thing. Yes, there's no question that Momy, alias Solomon, Levy enjoys life.

And when he said that his family are his treasure, he meant it. 'Thank God, my children are all settled and everyone is happy. I'm still working and then if, God forbid, I can't work any more and I'd be in a wheelchair ...'. If that ever happened, he wouldn't be able to enjoy the extraordinary close friendships with his contemporaries Robert Seruya and Abraham (Abie) Massias, to whom he is devoted. Massias told me: 'Plainly we love each other. Momy is a kind and very devoted friend.'

And Danny Anthony Feetham, the now the Leader of the Opposition in the Gibraltar Parliament, seemed to say it all: 'Momy is seen as a very decent man; as a flamboyant man; as a man who speaks his mind, but a man who is consummately polite to everybody; just a really, really very nice man. That's the best way to describe him.'

There might be something about the air on the Rock that brings such feelings of contentment. As he says: 'Let me tell you one thing: so long as you are happy and your conscience is clear, to hell with the rest.'